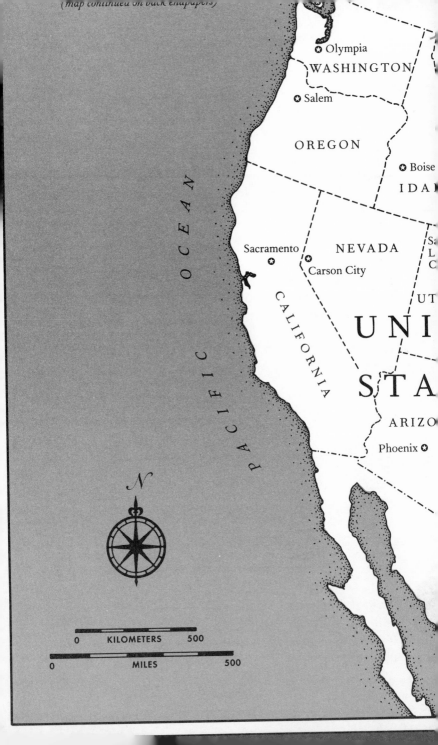

(map continued on back endpapers)

Olympia

WASHINGTON

Salem

OREGON

Boise

IDA

PACIFIC OCEAN

Sacramento

NEVADA

Carson City

Sa
L
C

CALIFORNIA

UT

UNI

STA

ARIZO

Phoenix

N

KILOMETERS 500

MILES 500

ZERO
TO
SIXTY

GARY PAULSEN

ZERO

TO

SIXTY

THE MOTORCYCLE JOURNEY OF A LIFETIME

A Harvest Book

HARCOURT BRACE & COMPANY

San Diego   New York   London

Requests for permission to make copies of any part of the work
should be mailed to: Permissions Department, Harcourt Brace & Company,
6277 Sea Harbor Drive, Orlando, Florida 32887-6777.

Library of Congress Cataloging-in-Publication Data
Paulsen, Gary.
Zero to sixty: the motorcycle journey of a lifetime/Gary Paulsen.
p.   cm.
ISBN 0-15-193093-7
ISBN 0-15-600704-5 (pbk.)
1. Paulsen, Gary—Journeys—West (U.S.)
2. Authors, American—20th century—Biogaphy.
3. West (U.S.)—Description and travel.
4. Motorcycling—West (U.S.)
I. Title.
PS3566.A834Z475   1997
813'.54—dc21   97-24799
[B]

Text set in Fournier Tall Caps
Designed by Linda Lockowitz
Printed in the United States of America
First Harvest edition 1999
A C E F D B

ZERO

TO

SIXTY

FOREWORD

I KNOW EXACTLY WHEN the genesis of this book occurred.

I was fixing up my old sailboat after coming back from Mexico and the Sea of Cortés to go across the Pacific and back around Cape Horn—where I think it is possible to look next for the grail—and I was alone and my fifty-seventh birthday came upon me.

There is in some strange way an almost sacred satisfaction in working on boats and I had let this one take me. I rewired much of the basic circuitry and added a single wideband radio, a second inexpensive depth sounder, tuned the self-steering vane, rebedded chain plates and bolts, changed the SON OF A BITCHING (I vowed never to mention it without swearing) galley stove for a new one, checked and tuned rigging, put in and aligned the new motor . . . the litany of endless work that is a boat. Each thing I did with complete attention as you must with a boat, forgetting career, family, everything; days on days working on the boat as if I were fixing my body, which in a measure I suppose I was, boats being such a complete extension of the sailor. I was lost in it, filthy and greasy and wonderfully lost and had forgotten all other things when my birthday came.

I hate birthdays—always have—as they measure the time of life, the ticking down of the clock of life and take into account nothing of the quality of that life; a kind of shallow measurement of the time to approaching death which cannot be stopped. Normally I ignore them but there are people who think they are happy and send cards or call, and so my fifty-seventh birthday was brought to me by a friend while sitting alone on the boat (which because of the repair work resembled the inside of a trash Dumpster) and I had to face the goddamn thing.

Here's how it went:

I am a man, in a time when it has become anachronistic to be masculine.

It's my fifty-seventh birthday and I have heart disease.

It had not and has not yet killed me and to my great surprise I am somehow two years older than Columbus was when he died. Twenty-two years older than Mozart.

I have accomplished more than I ever thought I would. Certainly more—considering the rough edges of my life—than I deserve to have accomplished. My children are through college and launched, my wife is set for life, and yet...

And yet.

Just that. An unsettling thought, like a burr under a saddle, rubbing incessantly until at last it galls and still it was and is there...

There had been a time when I was content. Not completely, and only briefly, but at least enough to settle, to accept, to live—shudder—within an accepted parameter. Then it changed and in the change I learned a fundamental truth about myself; saw a weakness that was a strength at the same time.

And in a quiet epiphany there in the clutter of the boat, varnish and dust all around me, I decided to write this book about a ride I took on a Harley-Davidson motorcycle that changed my life.

And so.

> From the sloop *Felicity*,
> berthed temporarily for
> refitting in Ventura,
> California, October 1996

CHAPTER ONE

IT DID NOT START WITH HARLEYS.

It did not even start with a motorcycle.

First there was a bicycle with playing cards clothespinned to the forks so they rattled when they hit the spokes; on a trip to Black Hill south of town you worked up enough speed on the downhill to get the cards slapping and buzzing like a motor.

Then there was a Whizzer.

One summer in southern Minnesota when I was just sixteen, I went to work for the astounding sum of one dollar and five cents an hour at a Birdseye fresh frozen vegetable factory in the small town of Waseca.

Unfortunately there was no place to stay in Waseca and since I lived four hundred miles away I stayed in Mankato with a boyhood friend, sleeping on a couch in his basement and getting up at four in the morning to hitchhike the twenty-odd miles to Waseca every day. If this sounds like a lot of effort it must be remembered that the summer before I had worked on a farm—sixteen to eighteen hours a day, seven days a week—for two dollars a day and a bowl of mush for breakfast, a bowl of mush for lunch, and a bowl of mush with a blob of lard in it for supper.

To actually make a dollar five an hour, forty-two dollars a week, a man's wage, amounted to staggering wealth. A hundred and sixty-eight dollars a month for— and this was the most astonishing thing of all—only eight hours a day and no work on weekends. It was like being given eight or ten hours a day as a gift. Like found money, like a present.

But hitchhiking as a way of commuting to work left a lot to be desired. Either I would get a ride immediately and arrive hours before my shift started or I would not be able to get a ride and straggle in after the starting gun. The foreman of my shift was a nice guy but the third time in the first week I was late, he stepped in.

"You have to get some transportation—a car."

"I can't afford a car," I told him, "or the gas to run it."

He pondered that. "You're over in Mankato?"

I nodded.

"Almost thirty miles..."

"I could walk it," I said. I was terrified he was working up to firing me. I would have done anything to keep the job. "If I hump I could do it in six hours each way—that would still leave me close to six hours to sleep..."

"No—tell you what. I've got an old Whizzer I'll sell you for ten bucks. It runs fine, clips along at about twenty, and gets right at a hundred miles per gallon."

"A Whizzer?"

"Sure—you know, the bike thing. You pedal it to get it going then cut in the motor and it starts and pulls you along..."

So started my love affair with two-wheeled motored vehicles—on something that looked like a fat-tired Schwinn bicycle with a little one-cylinder motor on it and a V-belt that led to the back wheel.

He had it in his garage. The tires were flat but they held air when we pumped them up. He handed me an extra spark plug and a new V-belt from a dusty shelf, filled the tank ("It takes oil mixed with the gas about twenty to one—less and she'll blow up, more and she'll foul the plugs"), and started me pedaling off down the street. When I got up to what seemed like wide open I pulled the little clutch lever and engaged the belt.

She lugged down and stopped.

"Choke her," he yelled after me. "Choke her until she farts and then back off and she'll run..."

I did not know exactly how a Whizzer engine would sound when it "farted" but I choked her and pedaled her and lugged her down to a stop. She would prove to be the crankiest piece of goddamn machinery I would ever have—choke her too much and she flooded and wouldn't start, don't choke her enough and she'd *never* start—and I would come to love her dearly.

I pedaled, lugged, and swore for probably two miles without a "fart" and was about to give up when with a mighty "Blat!" accompanied by blue smoke and exhaust dust and flame she farted (it truly sounded like a class-one fart), snorted a couple of times, hesitated, and putted into life.

There was a throttle lever on the handlebars, something the foreman had rigged up, and being what age I was and having what sense I had, I jammed it wide open.

We did not exactly slam ahead. The belt slipped a bit too much for that and the single cylinder wasn't much larger than a thimble. But as the putt-putt-rmm-putt-putt increased in tempo and became a reassuring hum, the speed began to gather on itself: six, seven, ten miles an hour and up, putting and belching to close to twenty miles an hour, a spoke-wheeled comet leading a blue cloud of smoke, heading for Mankato. I was mobile at last.

It was a glorious summer.

The Whizzer always started—if reluctantly and with a serious element of bitchiness involved—and rain or wind she took me to work and life without a complaint except for a new plug when the old one fouled and as long as there were no hills. If I started up anything steeper than a parking lot ramp, the belt slipped and she nearly stopped. I would have to pedal to help her.

I worked on the line where the boxes came out—one hundred eighty a minute—and pulled them ten at a time over onto a tray, which I then slid down toward the freezers. Boxes streamed out of the machine, I pulled ten over, then pulled ten more, and pulled ten more, and pulled until I could do it without paying attention and

had time to look around. I had of course seen Judy—
who had not?

Judy was an older woman—all of thirty—and had
been through a divorce and so was "experienced" and
"knew it all" and was therefore the object of countless
fantasies and dreams. She worked on the hopper that
dumped out tons of cut corn and shelled peas to be
squirted into the boxes to be prepared for the quick
freezer. But to see her working in a tee shirt that quickly
was soaked with sweat and stuck to her, to see her every
day and then one day to catch her watching me, was
something else. Finally she stopped me in the break room
where we ate lunch.

"You're the kid on that weird bike, aren't you?"

I stood taller and squared and said, "Not such a
kid."

"Hmm..." She studied me with open doubt.

I would like to say all my fantasies came true. I
would like to say that she took me back to her place and
we made love and she showed me all the things a sixteen-
year-old virgin boy lusts after, lives for, dreams to have;
that I touched her breast and she kissed me with her
tongue and touched me and the earth moved, but it
would not be true. Not a word of it. Yet sometimes what

actually happens doesn't matter; sometimes the belief, the desire, the dream become the truth and the waiting becomes more important than reality.

In reality, over time we became friends. In reality she *did* take me home—although not that first night—and fed me, and introduced me to her baby son, Robert. She told me that if I were older she would have liked to know me in a different way, the way I fantasized, but since I wasn't, she wanted me to be her friend and I was, I became that to her. We had picnics out along a river near town and I played with Robert, and she told me about her marriage and how it broke up and my fantasies about her went away—well, nearly all of them—and I found a new kind of friendship, clean and open.

Which was for the best because soon she began to date a man named Carl who worked at maintenance and I met a girl named Rosalia back in Mankato. Rosalia was fifteen and I met her at my friend's house. She went to a movie with me and then another movie and it became official and to me astonishing—I had a girlfriend.

So I would work my shift at Birdseye, then talk to Judy, and then jump on the Whizzer and crack the throttle wide open. In Mankato I'd see Rosalia, catch a couple hours of sleep, get up to ride the Whizzer back to Waseca in a stream of blue two-cycle smoke, and my life would go on. Judy would dim until the dream was more than reality and I would think—hope—that I had done the things I hadn't, and Rosalia would fade until all I could remember for sure was thick, short black hair and dark frames on her glasses, but I can remember everything about that bike. Everything.

A blue gas tank chipped and scraped where I'd fallen on it, the small Champion spark plugs, the slipping belt, the wobble of the front wheel, hissing squeak of the brake, slightly bent right pedal arm, rust-spotted front fender, two missing spokes on the back wheel and one on the front, and the wonderful light way she flew along the side of the road.

The Whizzer.

NOT YET A HARLEY.

No—too many other things to make obstacles. A life got in the way.

The army. Hard sergeants, hard words—the green machine army, and jeeps and tanks and missiles, noise, smoke, some men to love and some to hate, some men to live and some to die, that army. The marriage—young come-home-on-leave-from-the-army marriage, the learn-how-little-you-know-of-other-people marriage—but still no Harley.

Other bikes came. Bikes to learn on, training bikes.

A small Honda 150cc street machine with an owner's manual translated by somebody who didn't quite understand English—"It is necessary to get from plug the motorcycle a wrench special for the same purpose. . . ." Oriental-looking square front fender rattling, a large windshield bending back, and fifty-five tops, even falling off a cliff. A joke of a motorcycle that only lasted a few months until the new Honda 305cc Super Hawk with road racing short bars.

Some speed then, not a lot, and the bike unstable because of design and the short bars, but some speed, and when the mufflers came off and the exhaust was cut and tuned, more speed. No helmet then—nobody wore them—and there was some carnage but it was in some strange way acceptable. Jimmy Tort died when he flipped after hitting gravel, crushed his head like an egg. That's how they always said it, how *we* always said it: "Crushed his head like an egg." He wasn't wearing a helmet. Carl Kantine died when he leaned too far and snagged a foot peg, crushed his head like an egg.

Good way to die, we said, and, insanely, meant it.

We were too young to understand, too full of ignorance and piss to know there is no good way to die, to know that dying is absolutely and completely forever.

Then an English bike, a classic, a Triumph 650cc so beautiful it was almost a shame to ride it. Then a Norton, a BSA, and a Matchless, all beautiful and all just about impossible to keep running, all wired by Lucas, ever after known as the prince of darkness because of the unreliability of the electrical components.

But all remembered. Army forgotten, or close to it, and wives who became ex-wives, jobs about missiles and satellites and weapons that seemed very important but were really silly, and smiles and large eyes forgotten, all a haze now, all a part of the past, but not the machines, the cycles.

This one was red and that one black and the plug gaps were ten- or twelve- or nine-thousandths and the valve clearance was seven-thousandths and the tires were Pirellis or Dunlops and the best chain oil was (then) STP. You did this to stop a high-speed oscillation and that to stop a skid and you knew how many screws (for god's sake) it took to hold the headlight ring on a Norton and how tight a chain should be and when to change oil on each and every bike. Never motorcycle, always bike, until later when, finally, it became simply your "ride," as in "Good-looking ride, man." All remembered, all in detail, all perfect, and almost all else forgotten.

Some disasters. North of Hollywood, a large black man on a Harley hit a truck head-on exactly between the headlights, both doing probably seventy, couldn't tell where the man ended and the truck began. Good way to die...

A large white man, must have been doing close to ninety, lost control of his bike passing me entering a small tunnel heading down a mountain, lost everything going so fast he skipped *up* from the road and hit the ceiling of the tunnel, up and down that way twice, torn apart so bad you couldn't tell what part went where. Good way to die...

Hit a dog and blew over the bars and broke my left arm, clean, told the doctor to set the bastard without painkillers because I wanted to feel what it was like. Passed out instantly when the bones grated. Came to with a nurse wrapping plaster on the break...

Broke a leg when I laid the BSA over to miss a parked car. Clean break. Broke a wrist, broke an ankle, lost meat to road rash on skids. Buried Skeeter and Willy and Double Dick (lived with two women at the same time)—good way to die.

Still not a Harley.

Had some life in there, books and marriages and kids and jobs, years very poor but yet the bikes kept coming. Kawasaki two-stroke that would flat scream— clocked 138 coming down a mountain in a hurry to get out of a snowstorm, 138 with a woman on the back. Before the deadly donor cycles that came later, which killed so many young men whose organs were donated they got their name; that bike a father to them.

Bought a Ducati 250cc dirt bike when I didn't have a car, a home, or a job, and I lived on that bike, camping and looking at the country, watching the people because I was starting to write then, drinking, and read *Travels with Charley* by Steinbeck—worst thing he ever did, or nearly the worst—thinking that was what you had to do to write: travel and talk to people. I didn't know then that travel books were for when other things dried up.

But the Ducati was a traitor, a horrible departure from the normal beauty of Italian machines, and I left it dead in a ditch and hitchhiked to a town and bought a bus ticket—who knew I would one day be able to afford airline tickets? Left that bike and took a bus, back to work and trying to write at night, the hard slog that seemed to never work and never ended.

At writers workshops I would try to impart a portion of the dream that never was, never is, to all the people there who wanted to write but not really, wanted not to write but to Have Written; wanted to have the good parts (so they thought) but none of the bad: not knowing that it is the bad parts, the rejection and insecurity, the raw fear of failing again, and again, and again, that needs to be there, that is the engine that drives the writing. A friend who wrote well for a long time and published many books once called what they wanted pussy writing; writing lite, ersatz writing, retirement writing, I'm-going-to-write-a-book-someday writing.

I was there to give it to them, stroke them and lie to them and take my hundred-dollar check (but I paid for gas and food, sleeping in the car, which was usually free) and lose another piece of whatever dwindling integrity I had left.

We—my present wife, Ruth, and I—were very poor, living on gardens and trapping and hunting. I was starting to have some luck writing but there was very little money. A few books sold, giving me that thought that I had a chance at making it work. A man now, or pretending to be, late thirties. I knew I had to learn more—travel and speak at conventions and study and go to workshops—but there were virtually no funds available. So I found an old Chevy Chevette—brother to a skateboard—and fixed a bunk in the fold-down seat in the rear, and hit the road.

It was a strange life—a cross between becoming some odd kind of straight-arrow freak and a vagabond of the road—I learned a lot, but before long I felt lost, disenfranchised. If I was lucky I got home three or four days a month and soon became more accustomed to living on the road than living at home. I felt that I was losing my soul—that I was becoming less a writer and more a performer, and I had started to listen, actually listen, for the applause, had come to like it. I backed away from the lure as much as I could but I could feel my old life—woods and hunting, scars from drinking, fixing old cars and living, somehow, always on the edge of whatever I was doing—feel that slipping away.

It is very strange what saves a man.

I had a friend caught in the blind throes of bottom-drinking alcoholism who was going to kill himself, had the barrel of the .357 in his mouth and the hammer back and pressure on the trigger, ready to go out when he saw a spider weaving a web and became interested in it and forgot why he wanted to kill himself. Another friend, a soldier, was saved on a night patrol in Korea because

Chinese soldiers ate raw garlic and he smelled them coming and hid.

As I drove into Mankato, there was a Harley dealer, and that dealer saved me as sure as if it had been a spider or garlic.

I pulled over and parked, killed the motor on the Chevette, and sat looking at them. He had two outside— a red Dresser with a sidecar and a Softail, and I watched the bikes and let myself go.

Away.

That's what they meant to me then. Not to a place, not from a place, but just away. Gone. In and out of myself, away from what I was in danger of becoming, and I got out of the car and went to the Softail and sat on it and let it talk to me.

"You like her?" The dealer came outside.

I nodded. "What's not to like? It's a Harley."

"It's used," he said. "Just four months. Man had a heart attack and his old lady wants to get rid of the bike. I can make you a good deal on it..."

For a second, then another, I let it run in my head. Start the bike, the thought said. Start the bike and let it run. Just go. Leave the Chevette, leave it all. Ride.

For a second. Clean thought. Clear thought. Start it

and go. Never look back. Never see the same place twice. Just the wind and the sun and the motor between your legs. Cliché. Clean, clear cliché.

Ride.

Then I shook my head. "I have a wife, a son. I have to work."

He smiled. "You can still have a bike."

"No." I thought of where my mind had been. The lonesome and lonely roads, the sun out ahead, nothing behind. "No, I can't. Not now."

"Ahh," he said. "I see . . ."

And I think he did. There was pity in his eyes and I let it wash over me for a moment, and had I known then, known then how long it would be before I at last rode and knew about Harleys, I would have done it. I would have run. But I was young then and very narrow thinking and did not see the nature of the trap, did not know that my bondage—confining, crippling, and total—was entirely self-inflicted and that I could have stopped the jaws of the trap from closing then, right *then*, that instant and I would have been free.

But the thought was there, the dream. I turned away from it, from the freedom, and would not see it again until I was fifty-six years old and it was almost too late. Or perhaps is too late. But the lust was there and I am running now, coursing now, and will not know if it is too late until I die and still—please God—have not found the grail.

Then more life. The son grew, the marriage grew, the trap grew. I built a house and found that—why was I surprised?—Thoreau was right. If a man builds a barn, the barn becomes his prison.

I closed the prison doors on myself. Made the house and the family, and lest it is misunderstood, I have had perhaps the best family a man could. A wife who understands me and does not complain, a son who did not do drugs or run crazy and has become all that I could have hoped a son to be.

But I made a house and then had to service the house, and made a family and then had to support the family, and made a career and then had to furnish my career, the way a house is furnished, a piece here and a piece there, and thought and still think it was good and right to do these things.

Nor was my prison as onerous as many. I did not sit in a windowless office or have to listen to what I did not want to hear. I worked at home, doing what I loved to do—what Michener has called following "the loops and whorls of words on paper"—and not one part of it is possible to complain about and to my utter and complete and continuing amazement—and it *still* is unbelievable—I had a measure of success.

And I am grateful.

And more, still more, I have not been as confined as most men in their prisons. I have lived and trapped in the bush and have twice run the Iditarod sled dog race—indeed I have over twenty thousand miles on sleds—and have hunted when I wanted and fished when I wanted and played poker when I wanted and taken horses on long pack trips when I wanted and been able on several occasions to actually say no to some things and people when it was not prudent to say no; when all around me have counseled me to say yes because, they said, it would be for my own good—then I said no. *Then.*

I have had a life of such good fortune and seeming looseness that many who know me or of me envy what they term my "freedom."

True, I have not had to work in a bank nor become a lawyer and god knows I came to have some external trappings of what many term liberation.

And yet.

And yet...

I was never really loose. I lunged on the chain and stretched it, slammed against the pull of it but never could break it. Always it jerked me back until I would pace and walk the end like a cat in a cage—my own chain, my own cage—until I had rested enough or gathered enough strength or courage or desperation, *whatever* it was I needed and then out again. Running, pulling until I hit the end again, and again, and again . . .

But never loose.

Never the run.

Always the feeling of it, always the taste of it, but only imitation.

Only freedom lite.

Never the clean run.

Never the Harley.

YEARS LATER another Harley salesman, not like other salesmen. There was no glib phoniness about him, no checkered pants or white belt or lacquered hair or manicured hands. He was dirty with grease under his nails, had a full beard and almost no hair on top, calluses on his hands and scars from road rash on one arm, a face burned by wind and sun and a couple of teeth gone.

There were tattoos on his arms and backs of his hands and probably on his body as well, though it was all covered by a black tee shirt with the orange emblem and HARLEY-DAVIDSON written across it in large white letters.

He had ridden.

The display room was filled with Harleys. There must have been eight or nine new ones and perhaps another seven or eight used.

"I want," I said, "to buy a bike."

He perhaps knew what it had taken for me to come to this point in my life. All the living, the wrongs, the rights, the scars and the unhealed wounds; the near-divorce that it caused now. Many, perhaps most, men who came in had gone through the same thing to come to this point. He looked at me evenly, smiling slightly, understanding, waiting.

"I want," I amended it, "to buy a Harley." Stupid and simple and straightforward all at once. I had of course "wanted" to buy a Harley for years, decades. What I really meant was that I was "going" to buy a Harley. I had come to it in my life, had reached it.

The salesman nodded. He'd been sitting at a metal desk that looked like it came from army surplus. One of those gray things with the soft blotter top. He stood, smiled a flash of teeth, except for the missing ones. "You've come to the right place."

Here my ignorance kicked in. There were many different models—Softails, Softail Customs, Dressers, Sportsters, Heritages, Strokers, Shovelheads, Fat Boys, Springers, to name a few. Walking in and saying I wanted to buy a bike without a word as to what bike I wanted was like pointing at a menu and simply saying: Give me something.

I pointed at a red bike, glistening chrome and so beautiful it made me catch my breath. "How about that one?"

He nodded again. "Beautiful bike," he said. "It's a Fat Boy. Brand-new."

"How much is it?"

"It's sold."

"Oh." I pointed at a turquoise-green one with white trim, black saddlebags. "How about that?"

Another nod. "Great bike. Softail Custom."

"How much?"

"It's sold, too."

"Oh. The black one next to it?"

"Sold."

I stopped looking at the room and turned to face

him. "Let's do it this way. Which new bikes haven't been sold?"

He shook his head. "None of them. All the new bikes are sold, waiting for the owners to pick them up. If you want a *new* bike you have to order it ahead of time and wait for delivery."

Well, I thought, what the hell. A couple of weeks, a month. I'd been waiting my whole life—what was a month more? "So. Let's order one like that green one."

He nodded. "Good choice. The Softail Custom. Sit down and I'll write it up while you pick a color out of brochures."

He handed me some pamphlets with beautiful color illustrations and I pointed at one of the pictures. "This color."

He nodded and kept writing. "You have ID?"

I gave him my driver's license and he took information from it and put it on the form.

"How are you paying?"

"How much is it?"

"Sixteen thousand five hundred dollars."

I winced internally but I had known they would be higher than other bikes and I had spoken to a bank ahead of time. "Cash," I said. "A bank loan."

"Good. Good. All right, with taxes and delivery it comes to just over seventeen thousand two hundred dollars."

I told him the name of the bank and he scribbled it down on a piece of paper. "How long," I asked, "will it take to get the bike?"

He squinted at the ceiling, thinking. "It takes a few days to set it up with the bank and OK the payment, then I'll send the order in. Of course, we can fax that so that won't take any time... say just at three years."

"Three *years?*"

"Well, maybe a bit more or less. It seems to be running that now. Of course, in a year or so things might change. But new bikes are spoken for between two and three years ahead. Sure. Why, is that too long?"

I thought he was joking but he wasn't smiling and he had stopped writing on the order form.

"I am fifty-six years old."

He nodded. "Most of us are that old. Almost no young people can afford to buy Harleys. I just passed fifty-five myself..."

"I have heart disease. There is at least a chance I won't be *around* for three more years."

He laid his pen down and without batting an eye said, "Then you'll want a used bike."

I studied him for a moment but he still wasn't joking. "All right—do you have any *used* bikes for sale?"

"Oh, sure." He stood from the desk and looked around the room at all the bikes, then shook his head. "No, I take that back. There aren't any..."

"No bikes at all?"

He looked again. "No. Sorry. Oh, wait a minute. We took one in this morning. It's back in the shop being tricked up but I think it's sold."

He walked to a door in the rear of the display room marked EMPLOYEES ONLY and motioned me to follow him. "It's back here."

I passed through the door into the back and found myself in a small garage area. Gutted, wheel-less Harleys stood on stands around the room in various stages of repair. By the back door on an elevated stand stood a blue-and-chrome Heritage Softail. It had spoked wheels front and back, leather saddlebags covered with slide studs, foot pads and a motor protection (crash) bar, a small windshield and the wide front end with fog lights.

"Here, this one." The salesman stopped next to it. "But like I said, I'm sure it's sold."

It looked new and I checked the speedometer to

find it only had eighty miles on it. "It's not even broken in."

"No. The guy bought it and his old lady made him bring it back."

"Pussy-whipped," a voice said from beneath and on the far side of the bike. I leaned over to see a mechanic covered in grease. He looked like a garden gnome soaked in used oil and I saw he had two fingers missing. I noticed that the two other mechanics had fingers missing and then remembered the time I tried a brief stint at racing dirt bikes; a lot of the pit crews were old riders who had parts missing. Occupational hazards. "Waits three years for a bike like this and then he's so pussy-whipped he brings it back. Jesus Christ."

"Some men like to live that way," the salesman said. "It's what makes them move..."

"The bike," I said, bringing the conversation back to what was important. "Are you sure it's sold?"

"Oh—yeah, I think so."

"Deal fell through." The mechanic looked up again. "Couldn't get the bread."

"I'll buy it." It was out before I thought. I couldn't stop it. Years of waiting were in back of it, a frustration-powered blurt. "Now."

"I don't know how much the boss is asking for it."

"Go find out." He left but I stayed with the bike until he came back.

"Nineteen," he said. "Nineteen thousand plus tax and license."

I nodded. "Done." And then I thought of the first place we'd bought when we went north to live in the bush and run dogs; the whole farm, eighty acres and buildings, cost less than this bike. We lived then on two thousand dollars a year and all the beaver and venison we could eat. We could have lived for nearly ten years on what this Harley was costing. "Tell him it's done. I'm buying it. When can you have it ready to go?"

"Half an hour," the mechanic said, smiling like a drunk who has met somebody to drink with. "Just have to check her out."

"Come out front and we'll get the papers started. You'll need some accessories as well."

"Accessories?" I followed. "What kind of accessories?"

"A helmet. We've got the helmet law here. Do you have a helmet?"

"No."

"Do you have a jacket?"

I shook my head. Part of me now rebelled. I was in for the Harley but something in me made me suddenly shy away from all the geegaws. "It's the middle of summer."

"A jacket's good if you have to lay her over. You'll lose less meat."

"Ahh." I did not know then but within a year I would "lay her over" three times and all three times I would be deeply grateful that the salesman talked me into buying and wearing a heavy horsehide jacket, even when it was warm. "I'll buy the jacket."

"And goggles."

"I need goggles?" Jesus, I thought, I'm going to look like a geek. New leather jacket, helmet, goggles. All I needed was a silk scarf. "I was going to wear sunglasses."

He nodded. "In the day. But when you ride at night you have to have clear goggles—unless you want to wear safety glasses. I had a cousin riding at night without glasses and a bee came over the top of the windshield at about seventy and drove his fucking stinger completely *through* his eye. Like to gone out the back of his goddamn head..."

"I'll take the goggles."

"Gloves?"

"I'll pass on the gloves." I would sincerely regret this before I got home. At sixty miles an hour a grasshopper on the end of a knuckle was like a bullet—right before it smeared out and covered the hand with guts.

It turned out there was a hitch in the deal—something the bank called "a small ding, really only a dimple" in my credit having to do with my entire past, the fact that I'd been sued and had judgments against me and that writers in general do not make the best of borrowers.

We worked it out after I agreed that whatever happened in the *rest* of my life I would pay them first, but going back and forth took nearly three hours and it was near closing, close to eight o'clock before everything was at last signed and folded and put in envelopes and I stood looking at the bike.

My bike.

My Harley.

The mechanic had brought it around outside to the front after checking the bike out, changing the oil, and topping the tank with gas.

"You put the key here," the salesman told me, "in the ignition by the speedometer. You turn it on and the starter button is up here on the right handgrip. The

choke is here." He motioned to a small button down between the cylinders on the left side. "She'll need a little
choking at first, even in hot weather—just for a mile or
so until she catches up"—I thought of the Whizzer—
"but then she'll smooth out and you won't need it if you
start her warm."

He showed me all this but he did not start the engine, nor did he sit on it. There were ethics here that I did
not know yet. You didn't sit on another man's bike unless
you had permission and you didn't start the engine unless
told to.

"Have you ridden a motorcycle before?"

I nodded. "All my life. But never a Harley."

"No problem. You'll be in love before you clear the
lot. Just remember the weight. They're low and stable
but they're heavy. Let the motor do the work—motor
and balance."

He then turned and left, driving away—rather pro-
saically, I thought—in a small Honda Civic. The owner
came out—he hadn't spoken to me and gave me only a
nod now—and left in a Toyota pickup and now I was
truly alone.

The mechanic had shown me the gas valve, how to
turn it on and go to reserve if I ran out, and I turned it on

now. I put papers and a tool kit I'd bought—about twelve dollars worth of tools for forty-five dollars—in the left saddlebag, punched the helmet on top of my head, and straddled the bike.

I felt strange but in some way whole. It was like an extension of my body, and I cradled down in blue steel and leather and chrome and sat that way for a time, perhaps a full minute, and let the bike become part of me. I know how that sounds but it was true. I would meet hundreds of men and four women who owned Harleys and they all said the same—that the bike became an extension, took them, held them.

This is one hell of a long way, I thought, from clothespinning playing cards on the fork of a bicycle to get the sound of a motor when the spokes clipped them, but it had all started then. The track from that first rattling-slap noise in the spokes led inevitably to here, to me sitting on this Harley, sure and straight as any law in physics.

I turned the key, reached down and pulled the choke out to half a click, made sure the bike was in neutral, took a breath and let it half out, like shooting an M1 on the range. Then I touched the starter button with my thumb.

CHAPTER
TWO

SOME MOMENTS CHANGE A LIFE:

Actually running the Iditarod—not just talking anymore or training or sitting drinking tea by a fire and bullshitting about how it all will be but actually leaving the chutes in downtown Anchorage with your dogs in front of you and clearing town and into the bush. Then another day until the start-madness is gone and there's a point where you are alone with your dogs in the vastness of the Alaska Range, you and the dogs and the peaks— you know you will never be the same again.

The same with the Harley. First time with the

Harley. The engine jumped, ground a bit and then caught, throated into a rumble that came through the fluted pipes like music. The sound started in my stomach, or maybe lower, worked up and out through me and I felt the bike vibrating with eighty cubic inches of displacement and quick, before I could think, I slid the bike backward in a curve, surprised at the weight of it, aimed it out at the street, tapped it down into first gear with my toe on the shift lever, and eased out onto the road.

There. That moment everything changed. The bike held me like a hand, caught me and took me with it so that the engine seemed to be my engine, the wheels my wheels. It was singular, visceral, unlike any other motorcycle I had ever ridden. In some way it brought me out of myself, out ahead of myself, into myself, into the core of what I was, what I needed to live. And I knew, my core knew that I would never be the same again, could never be the same. A motorcycle. All that from a collection of bolts and nuts and metal and paint but more, more than that. A Harley.

I accelerated, felt the kick in my ass that only eighty cubes can do, the solid boot, and took a highway out of the city and didn't care that it did not lead home or anywhere I had been before, just that it was out in front of the front wheel, and I kicked her up to sixty, seventy and settled in for the run.

I ran seven hundred miles that first trip. That night I stopped at a cheap motel, called home, got up early and filled it with gas, noted a small seep of oil around the base of the rear cylinder—it was, I thought, after all a Harley—and then roared into the day. Mile on mile looking over the front fork, letting my ass harden off and fit the bike, into country all new to me. Some mountains, winding road, three thunderstorms, other bikers that waved in the low wave of Harley riders, my face burning and my body aching until the end of that second day, three hundred miles from home. I thought then I knew what I had to do to learn about this new part of my life.

I had to run long. I had learned that from the dogs. Whether it's love or work or laughter or pain or hate you cannot know it unless you run long, stay with it past the first flush, get over the mountain range and learn what it's truly like. The dogs taught me to wait—always to wait and go long and you will know, will learn.

I ran through the night, hot summer wind over the windshield into my face, the helmet off now and tied to sissy-bar backrest and to hell with the law; with hot wind in my face and over my head and the vibration of the motor coming up through the frame and slamming into my ass and the lights out ahead, I ran home because I knew what I was going to do.

I would make the longest run I could from where I lived in southern New Mexico, where I had moved when my heart blew and forced me to stop running dogs—the only way I could stop running them.

I visualized a map of North America as I rumbled through the night and thought that the farthest I could go to learn this thing was perhaps east, up into Nova Scotia and back, but I knew instantly that I would not go east. There were too many distractions there, too many people, too many problems. I could go north.

I could go to Alaska.

It was perhaps always there, the idea. I had run the Alaska Highway twice, carrying dogs up from Minnesota for the Iditarod, but both those runs had been a particular kind of horror. I'd done it in winter when the road was solid packed ice, the semi trucks were constantly coming blind around the corners, and it was always dark and I couldn't honestly remember a single bit of the drive except for the endless routine of taking dogs out to let them piss and feeding them and watering them and then driving another three hours and doing it all again.

I had done it twice but I had never really seen it and most certainly I had never seen it in the summer, when it is supposed to be the most beautiful.

I would make a run to Alaska and, I thought— maybe even come back.

I FOUND THAT contemplating a first run on a Harley to Alaska and back was considered by some to be unrealistic, by others to be extreme, and by not a few to be completely insane.

"You go to Vegas," one biker told me. "You drink and lose a little money and get laid and come back. That's a bike run. You know, a thousand miles or so. Five hundred out and back."

"But people make long runs on Harleys," I said. "They go all around the United States border, up into Canada..."

He shook his head. "On Dressers. Full-trick Dressers or Road Kings. You have a Softail. Man, you make short runs. Hold it down to seven or eight hundred for the first trip..."

"I did," I told him. "The first two days after I got the bike."

He shrugged. "Your balls are going to fall off..." And he was gone.

I studied maps and it looked to be perhaps forty-five hundred miles each way. Nine thousand all around. But I wanted to swing up into Minnesota on the way, which added a little over a thousand. Ten thousand miles and some change.

At five hundred miles a day that was only twenty days. Say one or two more for possible weather stops or breakdown and it was still only twenty-two days. There are some I know who think that twenty straight days with eighty cubic inches slamming your ass might not be the most serene of vacations but the Iditarod makes it at least more understandable.

First, the Iditarod changes all things for everybody who runs it. It is impossible to think short after running the race. Second, every aspect of running the Iditarod is so complicated, so involving, so obsessively intense—feeding dogs, taking care of dogs, taking care of their feet, *each* foot on twenty dogs, eighty feet, every hour changing booties, dealing with the cold and the terrain, constantly driving yourself—that anything less seems almost ridiculously simple.

You drive the bike, I thought, and you stop at night at some cheap motel and check the oil, fill it with gas, eat a bite, sleep, and ride again. What could be more simple?

In truth I think had I known how the run would

be—the rain, the pounding of the bike on my past-its-prime ass—I might not have gone. But ignorance is at least a form of security, if not actually bliss, and after having the bike checked by a mechanic with enough tattoos to make a mural if he'd been skinned out, I packed the saddlebags and bought a cheap rain suit, a roll of duct tape (from the dog driving days; anything can be fixed with duct tape), filled the tank with gas, and was virtually ready to go when Larry arrived.

Larry was a newly retired sergeant from the air force and had purchased a Harley when I had. We had met at the dealer's and knew each other slightly, but when I told him I was going to make a run to Alaska he nodded and said in a soft-spoken Georgia drawl, "I'd like to go with you..."

To the last minute I was not certain he would be going. Many bikers looked wistful and swore they would be coming when I told them about the run but for one reason or another they couldn't or wouldn't make it and I thought for a time Larry might prove to be that way. But he came down the driveway and turned around and I started my motor and we headed north with about as much fanfare as if we were going to the corner gas station.

CHAPTER THREE

"YOU LOOK FOR THE LINES," a sergeant named Stewart used to tell me. "Whether you're cutting meat or firing a rifle or fucking, there are always lines to tell you the differences and what you need to do..."

It seemed wonderfully erudite when he said it but then we were roaringly, fantastically, mind-killingly drunk in a strip club in Juárez, a naked lady with a boa constrictor dancing over our table at the moment—hardly the setting for intellectual thinking.

Or maybe the *only* place to intellectualize.

Sometimes I found what he said to be true. When

butchering game or meat animals there are places so obvious to cut there might as well be lines—where the back leg joins the body, say. In the Arctic when the night turns to day there is a line on the horizon so definite I once heard a musher say he could *hear* the sun come up.

My trouble comes in not always being able to find the lines, so that sometimes music can make me think of sex and sex makes me think of great books I hope to write and great books I hope to write make me think of eating a taco . . .

It can be that fuzzy and nonlinear.

So it was with the run to Alaska. It would be nice to say that it was all and only about Harleys and riding and scenery but the lines did not stay that defined and within a hundred miles I was thinking of poker.

We left southern New Mexico—near White Sands National Monument—and started north up toward Tucumcari, winding through the southern desert filled with yucca and sage, the sun cutting over our right shoulders, glinting off the tanks and speedometer back into our eyes. As we moved north past lava beds and small towns that seem to have been there pre-Christ, the country gave way to hills and piñons and stump cedars and we went through a small village with an adobe bar that made me think of the most cutthroat poker game I had ever played in, standing in a saloon in Santa Fe twenty-five years earlier at the end of a bar with four men and a greasy deck of cards. One of the men would later be killed in a similar game and I would not feel bad about it when I heard.

Remembering *that* Santa Fe game made me think of poker in general—a wonder it was, and still is, in my life; how it had moved with me and was still with me and as the bike tracked north, the pipes rumbling and Larry there in the rearview mirror and my back leaned back into the sleeping bag tied there for a backrest, I rolled in poker the way a dog rolls in something that smells and feels good.

Not penny-ante poker. Not strip poker. Not poker for fun or matches or bottle caps or friendly little nickel-and-dime-limit games that don't really count because they do not make your upper lip sweat when you call what you hope is a bluff but aren't quite sure. Gut poker. Poker with no-limit stakes, or stakes high enough to make you intensely focus on everything there is—and there is everything—in the game.

I first saw such a game when I was fifteen, working for a North Dakota wheat farmer. He was Irish and proud of it and drank with that same Irish pride. He had worked hard and raised a family and amassed land in a country where the soil is so black and rich it seems you can see to the center of the earth when you look into it. He was named Roy and had over three thousand acres of such soil. He could count on seventy bushels an acre, and with wheat running (then) a buck fifty a bushel, call it a hundred dollars gross an acre, maybe twenty dollars net times three thousand. Sixty thousand a year when a good man worked for fifty dollars a week, schoolteachers started at twenty-four hundred a year. "I make more," he told me once when he was drunk, "than a fucking doctor. *Two* fucking doctors."

He worked so hard I thought it would kill him, easily pulling twenty hours a day, and worked me and his other hands as hard as he worked himself—we got two dollars a day—and when he drank he drank hard and when he played poker he played hard. Stand-up-at-the-end-of-the-bar games—games I would later play myself—drop-your-guts-in-a-single-hand games, drunk games, mean games.

His wife sent me out to get him one night because she thought he was with another woman, and I drove the one-ton into the nearby small town to find him playing

head up with another man. They were betting their harvest checks. Two men, both piss drunk, elbows-keeping-
them-from-falling-to-the-floor drunk, betting thousands
of dollars.

They played draw and Roy won—he told me later
it was some twenty thousand dollars—but he had lost the
year before because, as he said, "I got drunk quicker than
he did." He laughed then and added, "I buy things for
my old lady when I lose. Last year I got her a dish-
washer, name of Carmelita."

I had never played poker, had never really watched
it played before this night, and I was transfixed, taken
completely by the game. The amounts of money were
staggering—tens, twenties of thousands of dollars. As
much to me then, as incomprehensible to me then as if it
were a million. I just saw the pile of cash and checks and
knew that at my sixty-two dollars a month there was
more money on the end of the bar than I would earn in
fifteen, twenty years. My whole life.

To do that, I thought; to be able to work as hard as
Roy worked, work so hard I would sometimes see him
puke his supper up because his guts were in knots, to
work like that and put it all on the end of the bar, bet it
like it was nothing, on a single hand of cards...

I wanted to be able to do that. Not only to win. Even young I knew you didn't always win; knew that indeed most of the time you lost. But to be *able* to do that I thought would make me a man; to put the money in the pot and look another man in the eyes and say those incredibly short and unbelievably focused words: "I call."

It has never left me, the nudge. Still hasn't. Later I worked and ran with a carnival for a time and there were always poker games going on in camp trailers or the backs of tents. Most of them were so crooked it was said you had to have eyes in the back of your head and they existed simply to fleece what the carnies called "the farmers," saying it about the way you would say "the shitheads." There were jars of clear corn whiskey so strong it would peel paint, which the carnies would give to the farmers until they were drunk enough that the carnies could peel cards and deal seconds and high-wire them and whipsaw them until they didn't know if they were coming or going.

The outcome was foreordained. The farmers would lose. They would get drunk and they would see everybody smiling at them and telling them how sad it was their luck was so bad but there was no luck at all. They were there just for the one reason—to lose and to keep losing until there wasn't anything left for the carnies to take. The games were watchable only to learn cheating techniques. It wasn't so much poker as it was a kind of butchery and once you saw how they dealt seconds and bottom and whipsawed, betting and raising on either side of the sucker to keep him calling, once you saw all that there wasn't much to learn.

But there were dime games played with new cards by the carnies between setups and before work where a young boy could learn how to play. I was paid thirty-five dollars a week with the carnival to help set up the Tilt-A-Whirl and to shill for a stripper named Rhonda. Out of that thirty-five a week I had to buy clothes, food, and cigarettes (Old Golds). And Butchwax to try make my hair lay back so I would look older and Rhonda would take pity on me and help me be a man—but that is for later.

The dime games were fair, or as fair as a carnival poker game could be, and completely and consummately vicious. They did not cheat—and considering that a good portion of these men had been in prison that was saying something—but they did not care if you were young and inexperienced and did not know how to play. They were merciless. "The best way to learn how to play cards," a man from New Orleans named (for no reason I ever knew) Wiggy told me, pronouncing it *caahhhds*, "is to lose. Nobody ever learned nothing by winning..."

And lose I did. On many occasions they took my whole week's pay. No wild games. Five- and seven-card stud and draw. (This was ages before Texas hold-em or Omaha—games designed largely for casinos to speed up poker and allow more players per table.) Dime limit doesn't sound like much now but then trying to live on thirty-five dollars a week and betting up to three dollars a hand (in seven-card stud with raises), it only took ten lost hands to burn off a week's work. A hand could be played in four to six minutes so the twenty, the ten, and the five I'd been handed at five o'clock could all be lost by six.

But I loved the tightness in your gut, the way your breath changed when a card filled a hand—all things I learned to hide after losing my pay several times in such short order I started to pay attention. I became if not cautious at least more thoughtful and I learned to watch other players, to learn their reactions to good, and bad, cards. I learned first not how to win but how to lose more slowly so I could play longer, and then finally, after many weeks of losing I actually left one afternoon a winner. Not much, maybe a dollar and a half, but it was a dollar and a half more than I had with me when I started playing. I had won. That it was just one time and one time after losing hundreds of dollars to get to that time did not matter. This time I had not lost. I had *won*.

I did not and do not like gambling. Betting on sports or craps or lottery somehow never appealed to me. I played the horses a bit because they were so complicated and it was necessary to study everything about them that it seemed for a time that horses might be as challenging as poker. But then I found that many—if not most—races are if not outright rigged at least shaded and it amounted to knowing the right people, the jockeys and trainers, and it wasn't betting so much as investing. Or stealing. So I left it.

Poker is not gambling. There is of course some luck involved—although much less than many nonplayers think—but in large games, where the limit is directly related to how much you cannot afford to lose, luck becomes less an element and skill becomes the reason people win or lose. It can become a very high degree of mental competition and in truly large games—no limit, table stakes, ten- or fifteen-thousand-dollar buy-in, where the pots can go sixty to eighty thousand dollars—the competition is so fierce that I have seen men, and sometimes women, force themselves into a kind of shock, eyes glazed, faces down, hands still, breathing shallow, so that their body and look won't reveal anything about their hand.

Those games are of course rare but there are many no-limit games with a two- or three-thousand-dollar buy-in and the pots can escalate—especially in hold-em, where eight and even ten men can play, raising with each card—to sweat-inducing size.

After my initiation at the hands of the carnies, my poker education flattened until I joined the army a couple of years later.

Poker and armies are of course inseparable and the games—relative to monthly wages—were large enough to make them good. Every barracks seemed to have a footlocker with a blanket over it or a bunk designated as the poker table and games went on ceaselessly and I won and lost about as much as I had with the carnies. My wage had gone down to seventy-eight dollars a month when I joined the army, and many a month I had to borrow from the "twenty-percenters" (men who loaned money at this exorbitant monthly rate) when I tried playing with a group of old infantry sergeants who viewed me much as a wolf would view Bambi. They played poker hard, drinking beer from bottles because they did not like the taste of cans, making small and bitter jokes about commanding officers ("pricks") and ex-wives ("cunts"), swearing in short, curt foulnesses with as much professionalism as they would field-strip an M1 Garand rifle, using the obscenities as a tool, a conversational lever to make a point. When they stripped down to their shorts—this was in the desert and the canvas Quonset huts we lived in were not air-conditioned—many of their bodies showed scars of such unbelievable magnitude and violence from past combats that it was hard not to stare. One man, squat, bearlike, balding, had the normal scars left by mortar and artillery fragments on his torso but on his left hand there was a piercing scar through the middle of the palm that looked almost like stigmata, a hole in the palm and one on the back. It showed when he dealt and was three-cornered and I asked another sergeant later what had caused it.

"In Saipan he lost his rifle and burned out a machine gun and a Jap came at him with a bayonet. He took the bayonet in his hand, pushed it over to the side, and killed the Jap with his other hand."

"Jesus. He looks so . . . so kind."

"He is now. Sweet as a puppy. Drinks and plays cards and spends some time in the stockade now and again. But come a war he's a blood-drinking mother-fucker. Good infantry . . ."

The sergeants were a good learning ground but they played a mechanical game, as if they didn't care whether they won or lost but needed the game as a way to fill time. I did not understand the poetry of poker, the lyrical quality of it, until I played with black soldiers.

The military had then been integrated for just over ten years and while there had been difficulties (as there are apparently now, especially for some reason in the navy) integration seemed overwhelmingly successful, at least in my units. There were thorns here and there, of course—crackers from the South who could not adjust, some black men who still felt unfairly treated—but largely things went smoothly.

I had four black soldiers in my squad and one of them became a close friend—a man named Strone, Billy Strone. Like me he was a buck sergeant—E-5—and he loved to gamble. He did not just play poker but gambled on everything—other card games, dice, sports; he would bet on which of two birds sitting on a wire would fly first.

But Billy loved poker most of all and he took me to black clubs in Juárez, Mexico, where they played gut blues and played gut poker in a room up in back. I drank then—which is perhaps why I don't drink now—although not when I played poker, and many nights I would sit and drink dark beer and listen to a woman named Henrietta sing. She was at least seventy, had no teeth, and she drank whiskey from a water glass and sang so beautifully, so soulfully, playing a honky-tonk piano while she sang, that you could close your eyes and fall in love with her.

The poker was in some manner the same. There were other white men there, but not many—usually just one or two—and consequently I was often the only white man at the table. They were all soldiers, some older but most young, and they played seven- and five-card stud, draw, and often split the pot between high and low. The games were fast and vicious but in a friendly way and the constant swearing—"comeonmotherfucker, *roll*motherfucker, givemeacardmother-fucker"—ran into a kind of music that rolled and folded on itself and became a form of blues, as rich and sensual as Henrietta's voice.

I think of all the poker that was my favorite time and I can close my eyes and still see Henrietta and hear the voices rippling and rolling the words to the song, the poker song.

CHAPTER
FOUR

RAIN.

We cleared Tucumcari as the clouds started to form and by the time we were up Highway 54 twenty-five miles, heading northeast up toward Kansas, it was pouring. It was the summer the terrible rains hit the Midwest, flooded down the Missouri and Mississippi, and we drove right into the middle of it. We had rain suits and we donned them and kept riding. The bike fit me now, completely, like a glove, and even in the rain the run was something to love.

At first, on the rare times when it would quit, we

would stop and take our gear off, then stop and put it on a half hour later and then stop and off and stop and on and finally we just left it on. I wore mine virtually all the way.

Roads were closed, bridges out, whole farms and parts of towns were gone and yet everybody we met—and again, we drove through the heart of the worst part of it—seemed outgoing and cheerful.

"Yeah, hell, I lost my house," a man in a garage in Iowa where we stopped for gas told me. He was driving a pickup and was filling his tank. In the back were stacked piles of empty sandbags. "But you know, it could have been worse. We can rebuild—it's just work." He smiled. "It's part of the benefits of living by a river. In good years we get good crops. In bad years we get floods. I just wish the goddamn politicians would stop flying over telling us how bad it is. I'd like to see one of them assholes down here helping me fill sandbags for a while. I don't *need* a shithead in an airplane to tell me it's tough when I'm ass deep in muddy water."

We cut through the rain heading north, pulling over now and then when it came down too hard to see, through wet-green fields of grass and weeds standing in water, fields they couldn't till because they were too wet to take machinery. The bikes never missed a stroke except that when we went through a deep puddle and the water sprayed up, it would somehow affect my turn signal switch and cause it to blink for a right turn once in a while.

It's just work. He had dirt under his fingernails and old bib overalls and a stoop to his back that would probably never go away. I thought he might be forty but he could have been sixty just as well. His eyes were puffy and his clothes dirty and his fingernails cracked and he looked like he hadn't slept in a week. But he smiled and said, *It's just work.*

He probably grew corn, I thought, alternated with soybeans. The truck was older and he kept it going himself, as he did all the equipment on the farm. He could fix an engine, weld, plant, harvest, make babies and raise them, and smile when a river kicked his ass and many of the people I associated with now in cities looked down on him, on his type of man.

In Japan they used to have a class of people that took care of the dirty parts of living—disposing of dead animals, emptying privies, dealing with the drudge and dirt of everyday existence. They were, I think, called *etas*. Without them it would all have come to a stop and yet they were reviled, as low a class as the untouchables in India.

I was once an *eta,* in many ways still am, and yet by some strange sleight of brain and hand I have been transformed into something acceptable (barely, I think frequently) and allowed into areas where I would not have been allowed in before.

I know a man named Chuck Parsons in Denver, an artist, a true artist who has devoted his life to his art—involving structures and people—and when he was paying his dues he worked for a time as a garbage collector, riding the back of the truck, picking up the cans. "People don't see you," he said. "You simply aren't there for them. They might see the truck or their trash can but they look right through you. They don't want to know you exist."

I was recently sitting in an airport with a young woman waiting for a plane and some soldiers walked by. They were also young—had the whitewall haircuts that meant they were just out of basic training—and she asked me what they did.

"They're soldiers," I said. "They're in the army."

"But what do they do?"

"You mean the army?"

"Them. The men in the army. What is their job?"

"They kill people. The army teaches them to kill people."

"No." Her eyes were wide. "I thought they like, you know, kept the peace and things."

"They do that by fighting," I said. "By being able to kill people."

"How?"

"You mean how do they kill people?"

"Yes."

"With rifles and grenades and knives and their hands, if they have to. With artillery and missiles and bombs..."

She shook her head and held up her hands. "T.M.I.! T.M.I.!"

"T.M.I.?"

"Too much information," she said. "I don't need to know people do those things..."

"Ahh, I see." The soldiers were then *eta* as well, somebody who does the dirty work.

I wonder what she'd say, I thought, if she knew I'd been a soldier and been trained to do those things, or that I had worked construction and farmed and drove a truck and spit and shit in the woods. Or that I had learned, fundamentally, of the difference between men and those who looked down on them when I worked in the mountains of Colorado replacing septic systems.

Colorado had recently changed their laws regarding septic systems and mountain homes, and as a result, many of these homes—expensive homes on five or ten acres in posh bedroom communities of Denver—had to replace their entire systems. At about this time I went to work for a company that did septic systems and push-outs for mountain homes. New septic systems are, if not always easy, almost always clean. You dig a hole, put a concrete tank down in it, run sewer pipe from the new home to the tank, and then dig a leach field out away from the tank for the overflow. There are "solids" and there are "fluids" that come into the tank and the bacteria eat the "solids" and turn it all into "fluids." With a new system it's all fresh dirt and the work is not offensive.

But when the system has to be changed, the tank that is pulled out has "solids" and "fluids" in it, and though pumped as dry as possible the old tank often breaks or flops over sideways so the residue slops back into the hole.

As bottom man—new employee—on the totem pole, I was given a shovel and sent down into the hole to clean out the last bit before a new tank was put in. I have done harder jobs in my life—hot tar and gravel roofing in August in Denver, chainsawing a ski area in four feet of snow, a briefly crippling and memorable time trying to carry a hod up and down a scaffold to supply two master bricklayers—but I have never done one so odious as climbing down into a pit full of human shit and throwing it out over my head with a shovel.

If that were all it would be bad enough, but when you pulled the tank in an old system, it left the sewer pipe coming from the house open over your head while you worked in the pit. I would go to each house—for some reason they all seemed to be owned by airline pilots—when we started work and explain carefully, in great detail, that I would be working down in the hole and would they please, please, *not* flush the toilet until we told them.

It didn't matter. Invariably they would make a "mistake" and flush the toilet and I would get the load on my head. My coworkers thought it was great fun—they had, after all, been there before they had graduated to working on top. "Man—look at the size of the sewer trout the grunt caught," they'd say when a turd, an actual human turd, fell on the back of my neck. "You could fillet that son of a bitch..."

The first time it happened I started for the house with a shovel—it took all three of the men I worked with to stop me—and when it had happened four times I evolved a new procedure. "I am going to be working in the pit," I would tell them. "If you flush your toilet I am going to break every window in your house." I meant it. There were complaints, of course, about the rude man working in the pit but the turds quit hitting me. The evolution I had undergone is, I think, symptomatic of *eta* in general. I had started as an average worker but about the fourth time they shit on my head I became mean.

This happens in a lot of what men are forced to do. There is a saying that a master bricklayer can build a great university but once that is done he will no longer be welcome in the building he has made.

Certainly in all the jobs that men and some women must do, nothing is more *eta* than that of being a policeman...

For a long period in my youth, I could not be in my home with my parents. They drank and were in many other ways obnoxious, and so I hit the streets and lived by what passed for my wits. I was exactly on the edge of being what was then termed a juvenile delinquent. I set pins in a bowling alley and sold papers in bars and hustled drunks for money and slept in the basement of the apartment building we lived in. The primary reason I did not wind up in prison—as so many boys who lived like I did ended up—was a big, tough redneck cop. He would also teach me many of the things required in being a man.

One night when I was going to break into a garage and steal a pair of old skis to hock, this cop caught me and pinned me against a garage wall in the headlights of his squad car. This was a small northern town and he worked alone.

"Well, you little fuckhead, what were you doing?"

"Nothing."

He put pressure on my arm, raised it up in back until I thought it would break. "Again," he said. "What were you doing?"

"I was going to break into the garage."

"For what?"

"I need a place to stay. My folks are drunks and . . ."

He pushed the arm up again. "I know your old man. He's drunk but he ain't that mean. Why were you breaking in?"

"To take a pair of skis."

"To *steal* a pair of skis."

"Yes."

The arm pushed up.

"Yes *sir*."

He let my arm go, turned me around. "Get in the car..." I started for the passenger's side. "Backseat. You sit in the backseat where the shit sits."

I climbed in the rear and sat there, looking at him through the mesh while he got in and started the car. I thought he was taking me to jail but he turned the wrong way and headed out of town.

"Where are we going?" I asked, but he didn't answer. It was winter, northern winter in mid-January and very cold—perhaps twenty below zero. I knew nothing of this man—the way I had lived I avoided knowing cops—but he seemed rough and I had heard stories of cops beating people up and leaving them in ditches. Six or seven miles out of town he turned the car around, backing and grunting as he worked the wheel, and when the car was aimed back for town he looked back at me.

"Get out."

"Here?"

"Now."

"But I'll freeze."

"What makes you think I give a shit whether you freeze or not? Get out and start walking."

"Walk where?"

"Back to town. If you keep moving you won't die."

"But . . ."

"Out."

I opened the door. It was so cold the hairs in my nostrils froze and the air caught in my throat and wouldn't go to my lungs. I hesitated and he grunted, not a word but a command, and I got out.

"Walk down the middle of the road, all the way back to town, and think about what I'm going to do to your young ass if I catch you stealing again. I'll be back here in this warm car."

So I walked, and he did not relent. I walked all the way back to town in the headlights, at first swearing at him under my breath and then more openly, and at last, too winded to swear any longer, I just walked, covering my ears with my hands—I didn't have a cap—and did, finally, as he said. I thought about stealing and that the skis would not have been worth this much effort or discomfort and that this cop was an asshole and that if I ever *did* steal again I would be more careful and this cop was an even *bigger* asshole . . .

It took over two hours, that walk, and I was sure my ears were frozen off and that he would take me to jail when we returned. But instead as we came back into town, near the grain elevators he stopped the car. "Get in."

I moved to the backseat.

"No. The front."

I climbed in beside him. It was wonderfully warm. He was wearing a leather jacket with a fur collar turned up and he had it open and seemed to keep his head tipped one way or the other as he spoke, as if warming his ears. Sitting in the front seat, the shotgun in its mount vertical to his right, his belt and revolver glistening in the light from the dash he seemed somehow...solid. Invulnerable and solid. Like a big mean rock, I thought. I wondered, looking at him out of the corner of my eye, how many men he'd killed, because I had no doubt in the least that he had killed some. Looking the way he did, heavy, confident, strong, tough as chain, it was impossible that he *hadn't* killed someone.

"Are you taking me to jail?"

"Are you going to steal again?"

"No."

"No what?"

"No sir."

"Then I'm not taking you to jail."

"Where are you taking me?"

He was silent for a time, then grunted. "Are you hungry?"

I shrugged. I was of course as hungry as a wolf. I did not eat well and was an adolescent and could probably have consumed my body weight every four hours or so but I shrugged.

"When's the last time you had a square meal?"

I didn't say anything.

"That's what I thought."

He drove in silence for another ten minutes or so and pulled up in front of a small greasy spoon cafe named Harry's Diner.

"Out."

I opened the door and slid out and followed him into Harry's. I had been there before, selling papers, but Jimmy, who owned the place—I never knew who Harry was—had kicked me out when he saw me stealing a tip from a drunk.

"J.D.," Jimmy said by way of a greeting. "Your usual hamburger and fries?"

"What else? I need to make a turd..."

There were two other people in the place, a young couple only slightly drunk—it was just after two in the morning and the bars had recently closed—and they looked up when J.D. said "turd" but then brought their eyes down and didn't say anything when they saw who it was.

"You got anything besides hamburgers?"

"What do you mean?" Jimmy stood by the grill. He had just put a burger patty on and it was sizzling and spitting grease.

"Like a meal. You know, meat, potatoes. Shit like that."

"For you? I've already started a burger..."

"Not for me. For the shithead here. He's a growing boy, needs a square meal. I'll buy."

"You mean really buy or like the burgers..."

"Not cumshaw. I'll pay for it. Cash."

"I've got some of those flake potatoes I can make into mashed in a few minutes and some leftover meat loaf from the special..."

"Yeah." J.D. nodded. "Like that. And throw in some green shit too."

"I can open a can of string beans..."

And I had a meal. Mashed potatoes, meat loaf, and

string beans, which I hated but felt obligated to eat, and a large glass of cold milk and a piece of only slightly stale apple pie for dessert while J.D. and Jimmy talked about a new barmaid at the liquor store who had what J.D. called "a number-one rack."

"You could hang your hat on them," he said. "And they wouldn't droop an inch."

"On what?" I asked. A full stomach had given me the courage to talk.

"Her rack," he said.

"What's a rack?"

He looked at me. "How fucking old *are* you?"

"Fifteen."

"And you don't know what a rack is?"

I shook my head.

"Her breasts, kid. A rack is a woman's breasts."

"Oh. I never heard them called that."

"Christ, your education is *definitely* lacking. You ride with Daddy J.D. for a time and I'll change that straightaway . . ."

And that was how it started.

I *think* we became friends. I know that over the next two years I virtually idolized him—even when I saw his bad side, and he had one—and I think he liked me as well, although more as a mascot or pet and sometimes as an audience.

It was, to say the least, a very strange education. I would set pins until ten-thirty or eleven at night—open bowling paid only seven cents a line but setting leagues earned eleven cents and in a very good week I could make twelve dollars working the leagues even though it was late—and I would walk the four blocks to Harry's when I finished and wait for J.D. He always worked the eight at night to four in the morning shift and broke about eleven-thirty for food.

Unless he was on a call he would come by shortly and we would eat. After that first meal he made me pay for my own but would not let me have a hamburger and fries—which I would have preferred—but instead made me eat mashed potatoes and meat loaf and string beans. I think Jimmy viewed me as something like a garbage dis-posal because he could get rid of the leftover special with me. The special was *always* meat loaf.

"It's the only square meal you'll get," J.D. said, "unless you eat that shit lunch at school..."

I shook my head. Mostly I wasn't *in* school—I think I skipped pretty much all of the ninth grade, which would explain my flunking it and having to take it over.

"So you eat this. Otherwise you'll be a *little* shit-head all your life. Don't you want to grow into a *big* shithead?"

After we ate—it cost me seventy cents plus a dime tip for Jimmy (J.D. made me tip)—he would fart and belch and we'd head for the car and start riding around.

J.D. spoke and I believe thought in clichés but he used them as valuable tools, both for living and for teaching.

"Don't get mad, get even," he told me one night as he pulled over a city worker or employee or official—I never did quite understand who he was—who had once complained, in writing, that J.D. was too hard on the citizens.

"Citizens!" J.D. had fumed. "The time I work I don't deal with *citizens*—I'm out here with the shit."

The official was so drunk he had to hang on his car door when he got out, hang there with one hand while he tried to get his wallet out with the other.

"Stay in the car," J.D. had told me. "Duck down so you don't show..."

And I did as he said but I raised up enough to watch. J.D. didn't even give the man a sobriety test. He walked up and pointed toward the front of the car and when the man looked that way J.D. kicked his legs out from under him and he dropped like a stone, catching his chin on the top of the door and cutting it so bad he was pouring blood down his shirt.

"Oh, my, you fell," J.D. said—and his voice actually sounded compassionate and caring. "Let me help you up." He did and the man stood, drunkenly weaving, and J.D. pointed to the front, and when he looked he dropped him again, and again he hit his head on the door on the way down. J.D. helped him up one more time and then smiled.

"I think this *citizen* has been celebrating a bit too much to drive, don't you?" The man mumbled something and J.D. reached around him and took his car keys. "I think this *citizen* ought to walk home, don't you? You can come into the department tomorrow to get the keys back."

With that J.D. came back to the patrol car, climbed in, adjusted his harness and gun, and we drove off.

"Revenge is sweet, sayeth the Lord," he said as we turned a corner and he accelerated. "Let's see if the cocksucker writes a letter of complaint this time." He laughed. "Fuck with the bull, you get the horn..."

He was, at the core of him, a very hard man. He'd

been military and been wounded and while there was something inside that made him gentle and soft enough to care about what—I'm sure—he viewed as a worthless street kid, he was essentially extremely hard.

He dispensed what he called "night justice." I saw him hit men—never women, he loved women, I mean literally loved all women—for no apparent reason, or put a wrist lock on them and bend their arms up in back of them until one of them, a drunk, pissed his pants. He would see something in them, in their eyes that I could not see from the car and it would trigger him and set him off.

But he would also use it judiciously. On one occasion I saw him answer a domestic call where the man had a history of beating his wife. This had been the case in this instance and J.D. took off his jacket to put around the woman—her clothes had been torn nearly off and she was battered and swollen blue—and he took the husband in back of the garage and with his nightstick, as he put it, "beat the living shit completely out of him."

I do not know if it helped the situation in the long term but it satisfied J.D. and the woman smiled through her bruises when he took her back inside.

Another night we were driving around at the time

the bars closed and we saw a man, clearly blind drunk, working down the side of the buildings and heading into the alley. "Another lost sheep," J.D. said with a tight smile, "one of my poor night flock."

We caught up and I saw with horror that it was my father. He had pissed his pants and was so drunk he was barely mobile and was staggering down the alley in the general direction of home.

"Ahh shit." J.D. recognized him at about the same time as I did. "I'm sorry, kid." He turned the car and headed away. "I wouldn't have stopped if I'd known who it was..." And his voice sounded genuinely concerned, not hard-edged the way it usually cut.

"No skin off my ass," I said, trying to be tough, but it hurt, seeing him this way. We'd never been close, my father and I—I didn't meet him until I was seven when I went to the Philippines—and for most of my life he'd been a drunk. But I knew how he'd lived and thought of him as a hero my mother had ruined and made to drink (I did not yet know that everybody ruined themselves, and would not know it until I had done the same thing). He'd been on Patton's staff, had been a mustang who worked from the ranks up to major and fought in Africa and Europe and was decorated, and to see him walking in an alley with piss running down his leg was degrading. "He wants to drink, that's his problem, not mine . . ."

"It takes some men," J.D. said. "Chinese have a saying: 'Man takes a drink, drink takes a drink, drink takes a man.' Some men it just catches and holds. Others it don't bother."

If you had told me then that I would do the same, would become a drunk with piss running down my leg, that I would sober up and in the last seven years of his life—not too late but near, too near—grow close to my father, who had also quit drinking, and that I would learn in those seven years all that he had to teach me on being a man, I would have thought you insane.

All I knew that night was the sight of him walking down the alley and the strange softness in J.D.'s voice when he spoke.

J.D. tried to teach me many things, and some of them stuck and some were based on a John Wayne approach to right and wrong that was almost too simple to believe in. J.D. loved the Duke with something close to worship. He never missed one of Wayne's films and would sometimes ask drunks: "What would the Duke think about you like this?"

They rarely answered, and when they did they by

god better be a fan or J.D. would "tune them up a bit," as he put it.

"I won't stand for a man to insult me," J.D. would say, "unless he's bigger than me and then I'll wait and get the cocksucker later."

"Don't borrow, don't lend," he'd say. "There ain't nothing worse than a goddamn twenty-percenter."

"Never hit a woman or a child, except to spank the child if he needs it or the woman if she wants it."

"Women like spanking?" I remember asking, intrigued with the prospect. I was a completely ignorant virgin in full hormonal adolescent bloom and anything to do with sex roared through my brain like wildfire fed by gasoline.

"Only the good ones," he replied. "They like that and they like ... never mind. You're too young for that."

"For what?"

"For the next step. You'll just have to learn it as you go. I ain't going to be teaching you things like eating pussy."

"*Eating* it? You mean you put your *mouth* down there?"

"That's enough for now. Look, over there, isn't that a new Ford?"

I didn't see the car, nor anything for a time while we drove around and I thought how sex, real sex, and not what had been stuck somehow in my mind, must be the most disgusting and wonderful thing in the world.

He taught me all the things I would need to know to survive in J.D.'s world.

"Always get even, if it takes you the rest of your life."

"Don't ever, *ever* let a son of a bitch get up when you fight. If you get him down, put the boots to him—it's *baaaad* when they get up."

"Never piss in another man's pond."

"Always have a bigger gun than the other son of a bitch—then shoot first."

"Women are the problem, not the solution—pussy always wins."

"The sun don't shine on the same dog's ass *all* the time. You hang around long enough, you'll get your day."

"Always aim a foot past where you hit."

"Nothing will ever love you like a dog."

"Ford is the best. If you can't get a Ford just kill yourself. Don't *ever* buy a Chevy."

"Live hard, die young, and leave a good-looking corpse."

He taught me never to sit with my back to a door or window, never to trust anybody I didn't love, and always take care of myself. He taught me everything but how to handle his death.

I was with J.D. two years. School was a pisshole for me, I failed everything, I had no home life, had no dates, never went to a party or a dance. But all that time a public librarian gave of herself and taught me to read and write and J.D. gave of himself and taught me to live and when I became seventeen I joined the army because it was, in the end, a way out.

I had been in a year, had gone through basic training and was stationed at a missile school in Fort Bliss, in El Paso, Texas, when I got a letter from a friend telling me J.D. was dead.

He'd forgotten nearly all his rules. A boy had "stolen" (taken without permission) his father's car and had gone off for a joyride west of town, pissed because his girl had dumped him or mad because he had a hangnail or no reason at all. The father called the cops and J.D. was just going off duty. The father was a minister. The kid had always been a good kid. What the hell, I can see

J.D. saying, I'll go talk to the little fucker, get him to come home.

The father neglected to tell the cops that the kid had taken a high-powered deer rifle as well.

J.D. found the kid fifteen miles west of town. It was deep winter and the car had slid off the road and the kid was standing on the other side.

J.D. got out of the car, the kid raised the rifle and shot him in the middle of the chest. He was probably dead when he hit the highway, probably didn't have time to swear or call the kid a little cocksucker, as I'm sure he would have wanted to do, didn't have time to get his own gun out, didn't have time to realize that he had violated all his own rules.

Dead.

I went crazy. I tried to get a leave to go back for the funeral. It had already been held but I planned on going back and killing the kid, finding a way to kill him; J.D. couldn't take his own revenge, I thought, it was on me to handle it. J.D. had become a father to me. I had to do all the things he told me and kill the little son of a bitch. But I had become married and had a kid by that time and thought of going to prison and what would happen to them and so I didn't go, didn't kill him.

But I wished I had, and still—in those times when I am alone and it is night and I know the truth of what I am and what J.D. was—I *still* wish I had killed the son of a bitch and if he has died I hope it was slow and painful and if he is still alive I hope he does die soon and it is slow and painful. The little cocksucker.

There. That was for J.D. And maybe some for me.

CHAPTER
FIVE

NEW COUNTRY NOW. The bikes running wonderfully well. I'd heard Harley horror stories, from the bad days when Harley had their troubles, of having to rebuild them along the way, but they were—and remained for the entire trip except for a problem Larry had, which was caused by an outside influence—absolutely flawless. Neither bike used oil, ran rough, or showed any signs of difficulties the entire distance (more on this later).

We finished in Minnesota and started out across the prairies, where we were going to stop in Wyoming and do some touristing near Story, where I used to live.

As we moved into North Dakota, it stopped raining for a day and the sun came out cold and crisp—for late July—and we had to put on warm clothes. I had picked up an old snow machine suit in Minnesota that I used to wear running dogs and I put it on and would wear it every day but two for the rest of the trip, and even then feel a chill now and again. I had assumed we would have wonderful weather but El Niño or the gods or an errant jet stream or just bad luck (I heard it called all of those things at different times) conspired to keep the weather cold and often rainy.

I had worked this country when I was fourteen and fifteen and sixteen, and memories flooded back as we rolled westward. I had been a runaway, several times, and once worked the beet fields with illegal Mexican immigrant workers, thinning sugar beets by hand, eleven dollars an acre.

God how they worked. I don't know what misguided idiot coined the concept of lazy Mexicans because the Mexicans I have known worked themselves nearly to death. I was not a big child and did not grow until I was in the army, but I had worked all my life and was tough for my size and thought I was tough and capable of hard effort, but I could never catch them. I have never seen anybody work like they worked. I finally worked up to a half acre, sometimes a bit more, per day, while they did two, backs bent in impossibly clean white shirts and tan straw hats with a fly switch hanging down the back, men and women and children, brown arms flicking the hoes to take every other plant out and leave room for the remaining ones to grow larger, flick-step, flick-step down the fields.

They adopted me. Many people seemed to adopt me when I was young. Some of the farms we worked had provisions for feeding us—metal pie pans nailed to wooden tables to be hosed out between meals, spoons chained to the same tables, big scoops of boiled beans with bits of lard and week-old bread; stale peanut-butter-and-jelly sandwiches. But you had to pay, as you paid for the hoe and gloves to save money, the money deducted from your pay at the end of the job. The Mexicans generally cooked their own food to save money—large metal potfuls of beans with any animals we could catch thrown in—and they fed me with what they ate themselves. They caught woodchucks and squirrels, with patience and wire loops around their holes to snare them when they came out. All the farms had hundreds of pigeons, and at night when they were roosting, I would climb on the barn roofs and break their necks and toss them down to men waiting below to add to the stew.

I never worked so hard in my life and never ate as well as those thick stews and freshly made corn tortillas cooked on a piece of thin metal over an open fire, the women slapping them with their hands and pick-flipping them over with the tips of their fingers, somehow without getting burned on the hot metal. I'd like still to be eating those tortillas, hot off the metal, rolled up and used for a spoon to dip stew out of the big pot...

I don't know if they loved me—surely they were very good to me and treated me as one of their own—but I loved them, as a family. Some of the young girls I loved in other ways, though the parents were too reserved and strict to allow us to be alone together. I had been in love many times of course, in school, or what I thought was love but I never spoke it and was too shy to tell the girls I loved about it. The situation was impossible then. I was a town drunk's kid, poor, I thought ugly, and so shy I almost literally could not speak to girls and the girls I loved were always the most popular, the most beautiful, the most unattainable.

With the Mexicans it was different. I worked with them, we were friends and I lost my shyness, and there were several girls, black-haired and beautiful-eyed girls, that I was so smitten with I thought my heart would stop. Though nothing came of it, finally, excruciatingly, cripplingly nothing, we could at least talk softly as the summer nights fell after a hard day hoeing in the fields, sitting by the barn or shed where we slept after eating. I asked about Mexico in horribly bad Spanish and they asked of my life in much better English and I dreamt of going back with them, going back to Mexico and living near a sea, always a sea with a small house and a beautiful girl with black hair and deep dark eyes.

Riding past the fields and rows of beets now, the rich black dirt as we left eastern North Dakota made me feel a nostalgia that was almost painful and I think I could have stopped there, just stopped and lived and . . . waited. I'm not sure what I would have waited for—perhaps for the migrant workers to come again and perhaps to see them one more time, to work with them, though I could not work as hard as I did then.

But I looked in the mirror and even with the reduction I could see the questioning look on Larry's face and I shrugged exaggeratedly with my shoulders and accelerated.

You are always alone when you ride. Even in a

group you are alone. It is perhaps one of the core beauties of riding—the enforced solitude. With the pipes rapping and the wind screaming—the constant hurricane—even with a passenger on the back you are alone. The bike demands it, demands that you keep your attention on it, and the noise of the motor and wind keeps your thoughts internal. The only time I have ever been more alone with my thoughts is sailing alone on the Pacific and in both cases there is an elegance to the solitude, a grace that turns the act of thinking almost into a dance.

Still a kind of communication develops—hand signals, a gesture, a weaving of the bike at speed, a thumb or, less often, a finger—and I think now that I wish I could tell Larry about what I remembered, what I was thinking but it would sound inane. To stop the bikes and say: "I remember working here when I was a boy..." would carry none of the sweetness of the memory. Larry would smile and nod in his gentle way—he is one of the softest-speaking and most gentle men I have ever known, this in spite of being in a war, or perhaps because of it— and we would be on our way.

I could have told him later when we stopped for the night, tried to tell him of the dark-eyed Mexican girls with smiling white teeth—I know it's cliché but it's so true—and he would appreciate that. But the bikes are not only creators, they are erasers as well. The wheels roll on and new things come. The remembrance of working on the farms would be lost a hundred times before dark.

Not far from here when I was a boy, hitchhiking west to avoid arrest on one of my attempts as a runaway, I rode with a Hungarian refugee who had escaped the Russian brutality when they brought tanks and took Hungary. He was a short man with dark hair and dark glasses and was driving an old DeSoto at great speed, smiling and telling me of the wonders of living in America when a pheasant tried to clear the road, came through the windshield, hit his face and broke his neck and killed him. The car went off the road, but the shoulder was flat, as North Dakota road shoulders tend to be, and the car simply bounced and came to rest in a plowed field. He was not breathing nor could I feel his heart, and in fear I ran from there, covered with pheasant blood and guts, and an old lady picked me up and I worked for her until I took off with the carnival.

At the end of that day, Larry and I stopped at a cheap motel. I had done all the camping I wanted to do courtesy of the army and over twenty-two thousand miles on dogsleds, including two Iditarods, so I paid for cheap motels each night, but I didn't talk of memories.

We cleaned the bikes and checked oil and looked for grease or oil leaks—though they never used oil or leaked grease (so much for the Harley myth)—and it kept us busy. Larry did much better than me—his bike wound up looking new each night. I sat and made notes for a book I was working on about the Iditarod, *Winterdance,* and after the cleaning and eating some canned beans and rice and doing the notes, it was time to crash and get some sleep for the next day's run.

I have always been amazed at what people can become accustomed to, how they can establish rhythms and make the most bizarre behavior seem a natural part of their lives. Running dogsleds is a good example. So is working in North Hollywood and living in a small apartment there while I edited a tits-and-ass magazine and learned to *learn* to write. Or being in a small sailboat on the Pacific. They were all radically different and yet after a few days they all seemed perfectly normal.

As though I *should* be sleeping in a snowbank and scraping dog shit off sled runners in a dark Arctic night; or that I *should* be interviewing a stripper with 46D breasts, which she flops out and shows me, as if she were a serious artist; or that I *should* be sitting in a space twelve by twenty-four getting the shit kicked out of me by high wind and twenty-foot seas.

So it was each night with the bikes. The Harley and the run became the center of life, the reason I existed, and by the fifth or sixth day I felt as if I had always been riding the bike, that other parts of my life had been preludes leading up to this venture I had to do to get ready for this run. It became perfectly normal to have the wind roar past my ears all day; as normal as running eleven hundred and eighty miles across Alaska with a dog team or rounding Cabo San Lucas with a boat or looking at a large breast held out for inspection or having a sergeant chew my ass for burning out a machine gun barrel.

When the desk clerk at the motel apologized for not letting us bring our "scooters," as she called them, into the room for the night it seemed perfectly natural to think that a person *should* be able to bring a Harley into a motel room at night. (For the record, if the doorway is a three-foot opening—as most motels are—and on the ground floor open to the parking lot the bike will just fit through, assuming you have standard bars and the foot pegs on your motor protection bar fold in.) Larry used to take his into his room at night and rest it on cardboard so it wouldn't drip oil on the floor and to be honest there were several times on the run when I would have slept decidedly better if the bike had been inside.

We crossed the North Dakota–Montana border early the next day and saw the house Custer and his lovely wife, Libby, lived in when he left on his last ride. From there we followed roughly the same course he followed across the rolling Montana prairie headed down and back up to the Little Bighorn.

For the past several years I have had death much on my mind. Once I was diagnosed with coronary heart disease—"the biggest single killer of men over fifty" or so prates every blurb you see about diet, etc.—I started having nightmares in which I died each night. The goddamn dreams came every night and I revived a procedure that I had used when I ran sled dogs, which was to "fake" going to bed, get right on the edge of dozing and then get up and walk around for a bit so that the neurons that had been set to fire off the nightmare would expend themselves. I'm not sure if it works but the frequency of the deathmares dropped and I started to sleep better.

Friends have died of heart disease since I was diagnosed (it's been seven years now and I'm careful about my diet—eat totally fat-free—and it has worked; I'm still alive) and it has led me to understand the sweet melancholy of death. "Everybody gets one," a sergeant told me once—he was later killed in Vietnam—"you just try to be the last one down." A death that comes from age has a rightness to it. I suspect it still sucks, as all death sucks—and what an apt way to put it—but at least you get a run at things.

What happened to Custer's men was *completely* wrong. Custer himself was an enigma—a very brave man who had fought courageously in the Civil War and who had built a large portion of fame on his ability to tuck his balls in and ride one inch ahead of the fireball directly into the worst part of the battle. He was imbued with what the army still terms as "Custer's Luck." Horses were shot out from beneath him, his clothing was riddled, men around him in the Civil War were killed in droves, and miraculously he was never hit. He is still the youngest general ever in the American army, and there is a better than equal chance that had he not lost at the Little Bighorn, he would have been the next president; he had a correspondent named Kellogg with him to get news of his victory to the Democratic National Convention that was going on at the time of the fight on the Little Bighorn. Of course Kellogg was killed as well.

While it is politically incorrect to express respect

for Custer, it is difficult not to admire his courage and in the end it could be said that he was given his measure of fame; more than most men are given. He was something close to Elvis during his time. Women came to his hotel rooms in New York, he was given locks of feminine hair, and his book, *My Life on the Plains* (which one of his men who survived the fight, a Captain Benteen, called *My Lie on the Plains*), became a best-seller.

None of this could be said for the men who died with him at the Little Bighorn. They did not get fame—virtually nobody remembers any name but Custer—and many of them did not even get buried. They earned thirteen dollars a month and many of them considered this to be a good wage.

They were largely Irish immigrants who were forced into the army as a means of staying alive, or getting west to seek their fortune. They were poorly trained—many of them had hardly fired their rifles—and their weapons and equipment were second rate, to say the best, and prone to jam and misfire. Even the hats they were issued were a product of corrupt military suppliers and the first time it rained they lost their shape and drooped down around the troopers' faces. Most of them had purchased straw boaters—barbershop-quartet-style hats—for a dime and wore those into the fight. They were small men—five two, five three—and light, because light men don't tire horses. (Custer was small as well, and very slight—his clothing would be too small for most women today.) None of them, not one, looked anything like John Wayne and almost none of them had any direct animosity for or reason to hate Indians.

We followed their path and in the afternoon went to the site of the battle, parking the bikes in crowds of tourist vehicles. I had been there several times and elected initially to stay with the bikes because we had all our gear on them while Larry went to the museum and listened to the talks, but there is such a draw to the place, such a quiet pull that I thought hell, if somebody is going to steal from us let them start now in front of all the crowds, so I left the bikes (nothing was stolen on the entire trip) and went to my favorite place, up near where the last part of the battle took place.

There are of course all sorts of stories and theories about what happened. Twenty-five years ago I went to the battlefield with a man named Allen Oldhorn, who was the grandson of Custer's Crow scout, Curly, who had witnessed much of the battle and lived to tell what happened.

Curly had taken Allen to the battlefield as a small boy and told him what happened. Allen went around the battlefield with me and told some of the things he remembered. "Men were killed there," he would say, pointing to a spot, "not over there. They came down there, near the river, and when they saw how many Indians there were, many of them tried to surrender but the Sioux weren't letting any of them give up..."

Allen looked and pointed and talked in a low voice and it was easy to see the heat and dust and hear the cries of the Indians and the screams and swearing of the troopers in his voice, see the movement in his eyes.

"Men were killed there..."

They have put small white marker stones where the relief column found the bodies when they came in. They are scattered over the prairie grass in a pattern from the river up to the crest of the small hill where Crazy Horse led a charge that came down on top of them and wiped them out. All in minutes, really—the whole thing probably didn't take an hour.

The white stones looked like bits of paper, which was in a way fitting because the relief column saw what looked like pieces of paper on the hill from a distance. It was the bodies of the men, starkly white with all their clothes stripped off, the bodies mutilated and sprawled as they were killed and chopped up, and it is impossible to see the stones, think of the bits of paper without being moved. I cry when I am at the hill, as I cry at the Vietnam Memorial in Washington and for the same reason at Gettysburg, where in a little more than one day over forty *thousand* young men were slaughtered; one unit, the First Minnesota Volunteers, had left Minnesota with over a thousand men and at the end of Gettysburg only forty-seven were left standing unhurt.

They were cut down, Custer's men, for no good reason, because a stupid government wouldn't keep its promises to a people who for the most part simply wanted to be left alone to live their lives. Custer himself was one of the instigators of the Indian troubles when he led an earlier illegal expedition into what we now call the Black Hills, which had been given to the Indians in treaty for "as long as grass grows and the water runs." Custer and his men discovered gold there and the word got out and whites came in droves, men who didn't care that they had to kill Indians to get at the gold, men who didn't care that Indians would kill them. (There are still markers in the woods of the Black Hills. Hike there and you'll come on a sign that says: "Robert Peterson killed here by Sioux while prospecting" or, "The Mackey party killed here by Sioux while prospecting.")

The government was of course at fault, has always been at fault in dealing with the Indians—or the Mexicans or the blacks or the Asians or (early on) the Irish or the Polish or the Finns, depending on where and when you were in the United States.

But the blame was not on those troopers any more than it was on the fifty-seven thousand men and women who died in Vietnam. It was on the political leaders—Grant then, who had arguably the most corrupt political administration in American history until Reagan—Kennedy and McNamara and Johnson later. They are the ones to blame. And the American people, perhaps, but not the men who left the small white stones scattered across the prairie grass. They are blameless.

Larry was very quiet when we were finished and we sat in a restaurant nearby and had iced tea and talked about other things, bikes and the weather, and how small the men had been and joked about Custer's jockstrap, which Libby donated to the museum, which also looked small—but we didn't talk much about the white stones—and I was glad to get back on the bike and be alone with the wind and the roar of the motor and my thoughts.

A strange coincidental footnote: When the battle was over, everything was gone—money from the men's pockets, watches, letters—everything. It was a mystery for years until an enterprising reporter found the stuff, which had been buried in a cairn above the grave of Two Moons, a Cheyenne chief who led the Cheyenne in the battle. The reporter was a woman named Kathryn Wright and she is my wife's aunt.

Another aside: My wife has a Colt single-action .45 revolver, the gun belt and the badge of her great-great-granduncle. The gun is in very good shape and I noticed that something had been ground off just before the serial number. I asked an authority on it and he said that that particular serial lot of Colts had been in the army, specifically issued to the Seventh Cavalry—the "US" prior to the number had been ground off when the gun was sold surplus some years later—so it's likely the handgun had been at the battle, carried by some of Reno's or Benteen's men who survived by hunkering down in back of dead horses and scooping small depressions (still there) with their mess cups. It is strange to hold the weapon and think where it has been.

In this place, this part of the country, Montana down to Sheridan and Story, Wyoming, much of the trouble with the Sioux and Cheyenne happened, small battles here, larger ones there, and for me, at least for the time, the character of the trip changed. I thought less of touring, less of the run and more of the men who had come there, both Indians and troopers, and because it was such a part of what happened, the country as well.

CHAPTER SIX

THE SCENERY WAS STRIKING. The Bighorn Mountains are among the most beautiful in the world with classically snowcapped peaks all summer as well as winter and beautiful rivers, and I had come there to heal when I first learned of my heart problem.

There is something very liberating about heart disease. You get a solid, rich copper smell of your own mortality and it's impossible to keep it from affecting how you live. Life goes on around you, people have all the things happening to them that they think are vitally important—car payments, careers, lawyers, awards, families—and you *know*, in your heart, that it's all bullshit. Heart disease gives you that freedom.

Life demands only one thing. That you live it. And the corollary is to do it the best way you know how. We are no better, nor worse, than dogs or ants or sparrows. All other things are, in the large scope of things, as meaningful and as meaningless as religion.

I was given this with my heart disease, this quick wisdom, and because I could no longer run dogs, the northern Minnesota winters were not nearly as interesting as they had been. I headed south but I missed winter so much that I decided to live for a time in Wyoming, where the winters were not as hard (I was to find this to be a bad judgment) and there was still some country to get into that hadn't been ruined by people yet. A side benefit of running dogs in the northern bush is that you learn the beauty of being alone.

I found a small cabin on the edge of Story, which is at the very foot of the Bighorns, and we moved in and I decided to explore the mountains.

I could not do so on foot—while the diet was working, I was still not ready for hiking above ten thousand feet—and so I bought a couple of horses, a thirteen-year-old mare named Merry and a black cow pony mutt-horse named Blackie. They proved to be as loyal and true to me—after some initial experiments to establish learning curves, theirs and mine both—as any dog, although they were not as smart. I had ridden horses all my life, starting as a child working my uncle's farms in Minnesota and North Dakota on workhorses. Riding the teams when they brought hay in from the fields as they plodded along and spending summer afternoons dozing on their backs with a straw in my mouth and talking about everything and nothing with my cousins while the giant horses grazed, oblivious to our weight, and it was here, really, that I decided to be a storyteller. I was thirteen and on a hot summer day with popcorn clouds I made up a story about riding a horse a long distance and meeting a girl—always there was a girl—who thought much of me because I was on a horse, a cowboy. When I stopped talking just before the girl would have given me a kiss in gratitude for saving her (cat, calf, puppy, mother, baby sister, or brother—choose one) one of my cousins said: "Then what happened?"

"Nothing," I answered. "It's just a story I made up."

"That doesn't matter a pink turd," he said. "It's still a good story and if you don't tell how it ends I'm going to whip you."

I found he was right—it really doesn't matter a pink turd and only the story counts—and many years later when I started to write about things that had really happened to me it was the same; the story mattered more than the event in some way.

Later I learned of Shetland ponies, and what miserable little mean bastards they could be—I *still* have scars from the bite marks—and glitter horses like palaminos and Appaloosas and quarter horses and walkers. Once drunk in Montana I even tried a brief stint at bareback bronc riding, using a borrowed rig, and have always had a kind of respect for what horses can give if not the love I would come to have for dogs. I had amassed some knowledge of them by the time I came to Merry and Blackie, or thought I had (they were to teach me much more, about horses and myself). But I had never worked with a packhorse.

I trained Blackie to carry a packsaddle. This did not go nearly as smoothly as that sentence implies. Blackie had never been packed before and while he was a steady horse with a great heart he also was eleven years old and had very set ideas on what should or should not be put on his back. A saddle was fine. A person was fine. A person and a saddle with a yellow rain slicker—if it did not come untied and flap in a wind—were fine. I even rode him out a ways and fired a .357 Magnum off his back and *that* was fine.

A packsaddle was *not* fine.

And if it had a bunch of gear in it—stoves, pots and pans, changes of clothing, a pad for writing, and some cans of beans and rice—it was doubly cursed.

I had come from the smooth grace of dogsleds, carrying gear on long runners, where even if the dogs rebelled or you hit a tree, the damage to equipment was minimal. I was most decidedly not prepared for the force of Blackie's reaction. To be sure there was a warning. He accepted the packsaddle and the canvas panniers but when I started putting equipment in the bags and it rattled a bit, his eyes grew wide and his nostrils flared. I saw this but decided it was momentary nervousness.

The pack was off balance but I had talked to an old packsaddle expert named Jack who had packed all over the Bighorns and he said simply equal it out with rocks. A man of few words and unconfused concepts, Jack had the rare experience of riding a horse in the high country when the horse was hit by lightning.

"The horse didn't like it much," he said. "It kilt him."

I equalized the load with rocks and still Blackie

stood for it. Then one of the stones settled a bit and rattled against a pan or the side of the stove.

I have never seen anything like it. Pots and pans flew through the air along with bedding and cans of fat-free chili and in a manic rage he reduced a small Coleman stove to its molecular base.

Then he stood, still tied to the tree, quietly breathing through wide nostrils while I gathered up what hadn't been totally destroyed and repacked and he went nuclear again. In all we did it four times before he accepted the load but once he did he was good from then on and the mare—elegant, fast, and fine-boned—was glad to pull him.

Leaving on the trail out of Story we packed all over the Bighorns, using old trails and in some places no trail at all, that whole summer. Much of the country we covered had been central in the Indian troubles with the Sioux and Cheyenne and on one of the trips I came on an old .45–70 cartridge case by a tree. The troopers with Custer had been issued .45–70s, as had most of the army at that time, and the Indians had come up into the Bighorns after the Custer battle to evade capture and I wondered if this shell had been taken from some dead trooper along with his rifle.

During the Second World War a B-17 had plowed into one of the peaks in the Bighorns and I tried to get up to it with the horses but couldn't because it seemed the terrain was too rough for the horses. I did however meet one Jimmy Huggins, an old cowboy who had brought the bodies of the crew out and who stays in the summer in a cabin by a lake in the high country to open and close the spillway and let water out for irrigating hay fields in the prairie below. I stopped there for two nights hoping some snow would melt out of a pass and let me through (it didn't; I was to find later it had been over forty-two *feet* deep), and Jimmy was kind enough to put me up.

He was a singular man. He would sit smoking an old pipe, giving himself insulin injections, and talk in a low voice about the western actor Ben Johnson (whom he said he knew and respected a great deal; he said Ben lived his life on handshakes and none of "all this lawyer bullshit") and pack trips with thirty packhorses being pulled by one man and hunts in the high country that found record elk and horses so good they were "god-damn near perfect" and so bad they "ought to be shot down like a bad dawg."

He made pancakes on a wood cookstove and I had some canned potatoes and tried to make a stew that was barely edible but he ate it and politely complimented me on it and told the story of getting the dead crew of the bomber off the mountain.

He could not get packhorses up there for I think two years because of the weather and rough country—it was easily as bad as anything I had seen in two Iditarods—and I thought of the bodies of the crew and said they must have been in rough shape by that time.

"Naww, hell, it was so cold the meat was still good on 'em..."

Tough. In Alaska the highest compliment I ever heard about a man—or a woman—was just that: He's tough. It was not given lightly, not even about all the people who run the Iditarod. Only a few get described that way. It meant, simply, that the person could take it. Nothing phony or showy, not a flashy hero or publicity seeker—just able to take whatever comes and roll with it or die. I met a musher in Alaska who had been taking a dog team with his baby in the sled across thirty miles of rough country to get to a trading post. A moose attacked him, killed half his team, kicked the baby (miraculously without harming it) off into a snowbank, stomped the sled into junk, and then went on its way. This man gathered up the baby, four dogs that could still pull, hooked them up to the plastic sheeting that had been on the bottom of the sled, lay down with his baby sheltered beneath him and slid like that on his stomach through twenty miles of mountains. That kind of tough. Jimmy was/is that tough.

I was not done with horses yet and took them with me when I left Wyoming and headed down to New Mexico—after two successive Wyoming snowfalls of over twenty inches in ten days. Blackie again provided me with a lesson in both patience and stubbornness. He apparently had never been trailered (the man who sold him to me rode him to deliver him—a telltale sign I should have seen), or had something bad, very bad happen with a trailer or, apparently, thought they might be the spawn of Satan. I bought an old two-horse trailer to take the horses down to New Mexico—where it doesn't snow quite as much in such a short time—and found that Blackie didn't do trailers.

I was for a moment stymied. I knew what to do with stubborn dogs, how to work with them and get them to do what you wish, but a horse, Blackie, weighed close on to eight hundred pounds. If he didn't want to do something, he didn't do it, and I couldn't pick him up and throw him into the trailer.

Jack, the old cowboy who had been on the horse hit by lightning, lived nearby and he happened by about the time I was standing looking at Blackie standing looking at the trailer. "He don't want to get in," Jack said.

"I know. I don't know what to do."

"Wrench him."

"I beg your pardon?"

"You got to wrench him. Get a wrench and pull him in."

With that Jack left and I was perplexed until I decided he'd meant *winch* instead of *wrench*, which was good because I had no earthly idea of how you would apply a wrench to Blackie, unless, I thought, it was a very big wrench and you took one hell of a swing and...

But a winch might do it. I had an old come-along in the pickup that I'd used to unstick trucks when I was running dogs and I rigged it to the truck bumper and ran it through the front trailer window and out the back about twenty feet and hooked it to Blackie's halter.

He was always passive—the discussion about the packsaddle was the lone exception—and he stood quietly now while I tightened his halter so it couldn't possibly come off. I then made a great show of putting some oats in a pan in the feeding area at the front and inside the trailer. This had no effect—it hadn't worked in the past either but I thought it might be some added incentive—so I went to the come-along and took up the slack.

I thought that if I just started the process and applied pressure he would get the idea and "come along" into the trailer.

I was wrong. He stood solid, braced.

I cranked some more on the handle.

No movement.

More notches clicked.

Nothing.

It was a strong come-along. I had used it to *lift* dead horses people had given me for dog food when I had sled dogs and I pointedly reminded Blackie of this now. "You can't win," I told him. "I have technology and science and leverage. You're a horse." I took a deep breath and heaved another two notches on the ratchet handle and he still stood there.

Jack came by again just then.

"That horse has a long neck," he said.

"He still won't come into the trailer."

Jack went around in back of Blackie and did something with his hand that I couldn't see and Blackie exploded forward, slammed up into the trailer, and started eating oats.

"What did you do?" I asked.

"Hepped him make up his mind."

To this day I don't know what Jack did and he has passed on so I'll never know. Blackie is still reluctant about getting into a trailer but if I get the come-along and click the ratchet, just once, he looks back at his ass and jumps right in.

Since diagnosed with heart disease I have seen cliff dwellings and deserts and mountains, have ridden with the ghosts of famous Sioux like Crazy Horse and the dead soldiers who fought him; of Apaches and black Tenth Cavalry troopers who hunted them; have dodged bear and been hit by snakes and fallen down mountains and swum rivers and been knocked down by flash floods and seen sunsets and dawns that no man, ever, has seen before or will see again in the same way or place; have heard coyotes and chased antelope and deer and watched desert storms march across the world and lain under stars so bright and clear you could *see* the life in them and listened to stories from Jimmy Huggins in a place that hasn't changed since, as Jimmy said, "God was a pup."

And all of this was from the horses; from Merry and

Blackie. They gave me a chance to see and be more at a time when many men—some of them dear and good friends of mine—simply lay down and died.

The horses saved me then as surely as the Harley did now.

CHAPTER
SEVEN

WE WERE WELL BROKEN IN NOW—that was the feeling I had and I think that Larry felt the same. Our cherry was gone. We had done some seventeen hundred miles in what one farmer told me was "the goddamndest goddamn weather I ever goddamn saw," and there was nothing left to break in.

We started north out of Sheridan in rain, back past the Custer battlefield and up into Montana. The bikes seemed to feel a change and nosed into the new country with a gleeful roar that caused cows to jump as we passed them in the prairie. This might be because we had both removed the factory pipes that came with the bike and put on resonators. This for two reasons: First, it was supposed to improve power and fuel efficiency—in my case it did not—but also these were, after all, Harleys. Harleys are about sound, a certain sound, and it doesn't come from stifled pipes. It isn't just volume—although there is some of that—but the gut-rumbling roll of it. They say of pilots that if they are near an airfield they cannot keep from watching a plane land or take off. Harley riders are the same when a Harley goes by—I have never seen one who didn't turn to watch until the sound was gone. (As this is being written Harley-Davidson is trying to get a patent on the distinctive Harley sound.)

It was in here, Montana leading up into Canada, that I really started to notice the effect of the Harley mystique. I had seen it before to a certain degree in New Mexico and Texas, and even in the Midwest. And god knows it affected me—and still does—as much as anybody.

There is something fundamentally American about a Harley. The way they look and sound, the size and mass of them, the care (now, if not so much in the past) taken in their manufacture mixes the feeling of the Wright brothers with Barney Oldfield and Eddie Rickenbacker and Marlon Brando and leather helmets and goggles and chaps and a measure of sex and intense wanderlust into a big ball of empathy that is almost overwhelming.

That's part of it. But only part. The other aspect, and perhaps more important, is visceral and thick and heavy and very, very sexual. I have on many occasions actually had women say: "Ohhhh, you've got a Harley..." in as frank a display of sexuality as any I've seen (and this includes editing that tits-and-ass magazine in Hollywood for a year). This feeling of the bike, the sexuality combined with the patriotic and aesthetic mystique, makes a brew so heady that it becomes overwhelming, almost narcotic. This is enhanced when you ride—the thunder, the grace of it—and it becomes very difficult, almost impossible to come down.

It is interesting to watch a Harley showroom on a weekend day. Men come in and three feet inside the door they stop and a kind of stunned, glazed look comes into their eyes as they walk around and touch the bikes, just touch them, and dream and hope and wish.

Many, many more want Harleys than can have them—hence the three-year waiting period for a new one—and this desire became more and more evident as we started our run north. There are of course stories about some dealers shipping all their used bikes to Europe, where it is rumored that a Harley might sell for twice and even three times its face value. There is perhaps some truth in this—although I have not been able to find a dealer who does this—and it has given rise to the latest techno myth: that a couple of Germans came over here, bought used Harleys and toured America and Canada, then took the bikes back to Germany, where they sold them for enough to cover the original cost of the bikes, paid for the whole trip and shipping costs, and made a handsome profit besides. This might be one of those stories that belongs with the three- or four- or five-hundred-mile-per-gallon carburetor the car companies have and are keeping to themselves because ordered to do so by the oil companies. Or the one about the spacemen's bodies in Roswell. I cannot find the spacemen or the carburetors or the two German men who were supposed to make so much money on their Harleys but the story persists.

True or not, the bikes caused more comment the farther north we went. We crossed the border into Canada and started up across the long flats of the Canadian prairie to get to Dawson Creek, where the

Alaska Highway officially starts, and every stop for gas or to piss or to buy a Coke seemed to bring people out to the bikes. They would stand and look at them, touch them, ask where we'd come from and how it was to ride them.

The most poignant moment for me came in a small motel in Dawson Creek. We'd stopped so Larry could get a new rear tire at (I think) a Yamaha dealer there and we got a room in an inexpensive roadside motel. After we got the tire we were sitting outside the rooms cleaning our bikes. I had discovered what I thought to be an oil leak (it wasn't, just some road oil that splashed up) and I was down beneath the bike when I heard a small boy come up to Larry.

"Hi," he said.

"Hello." Larry stopped cleaning his bike for a moment.

"That's sure a pretty bike."

"Thank you."

The boy touched the seat and the tank, put his hand on the grip and hesitated and I thought he was going to ask to sit on it; some of them do, though most seem to think it a kind of violation. Instead he sighed and smiled a short smile.

"Do you have a picture of your motorcycle I could have?"

And what made it perfect was that Larry actually had a picture of the bike and he found it and gave it to the boy, who stood looking down at it and the bike for a moment, comparing them, before running to his parents three rooms down to show them the photo.

Women became part of the run then as well. We saw no women hitchhiking in the United States but as we crossed into Canada there were college girls hitchhiking all over the place. It makes a hell of a statement about the U.S.—the fear that women must have and the dangers they face and how simply crossing a border can change things so much. Ottawa, Canada, has six homicides a year; Washington, D.C., has nearly that many each *night*. We live in a violent country in a violent time and it has sadly become accepted that there are some seemingly safe places it is not safe to go, especially if you are a woman. I wonder what J.D. would have thought of that, how he would have taken it if someone had told him there were places he could not be, where a woman would not be safe. He had had no illusions, certainly, and had fought in Korea and knew of that form of evil but still the idea of bowing to crime rather than facing it and kicking its ass (as he would put it) would be against how he thought the World Should Be. (An interesting secondary indication of the difference between the two countries: In the United States I don't think I saw a highway sign without a bullet hole in it; in Canada I never saw a sign *with* one.)

Larry was newly single and I noticed his bike slow and drop back as we passed hitchhiking girls and they smiled and waved at us and watched us until we were out of sight and he would smile at them and me and wave back but did not pull over. We would stop for gas or a cup of coffee in a cafe and talk of the girls:

"Did you see them?" Larry would ask.

"Yes..."

"They sure were pretty."

"Yes..."

"They waved back at me."

"I saw..."

And then we would ride again and I would continue the riding conversation in my mind, talking of women I had known as if Larry were there talking with me. I told him of Rhonda, who was the stripper with the carnival I ran off with when I was fifteen. Her husband was named Tucker and he ran the Tilt-A-Whirl and his brother named Billy was the sideshow geek. Billy would cover his bald head and face with brown shoe polish and pretend to be a wild man from Borneo and bite the heads off live chickens and splatter the blood on the farmers standing around the cage. On a good night he'd get two or three fainters and a couple of pukers.

Rhonda was forty and more, a slightly heavy blond with hard eyes and a mouth worse than many sergeants I knew, but she was kind and very generous and took me into their little camp trailer when Tucker wasn't around and showed me things I had only dreamt of before then. I would learn later the truth: of hormones and intensity of contact and much later of the ache that comes with love, first puppy love, and then older love, and at last real love, but with Rhonda it was not love, though I thought I loved her more than life itself, but rather a master teaching a pupil and I hope all the good things she ever wanted came to her.

Sex I would not learn the truth of until I came to know prostitutes. No. Whores. They did not call themselves prostitutes but whores and were not to be pitied nor did they consider themselves to be exploited—though I'm sure they were. I had strange relationships with many whores and what made them strange is that I have never slept with nor been intimate with one—they were not sexually attractive to me—but rather became friends with them through other friends and poker.

It started in the army. In some of the whorehouses in Juárez there were continual floating poker games. These were always gut poker, where you had to watch your cards and your ass, but often there were drunks playing and drunks playing poker are about as close to a payday as you can get. So I would go with army buddies when they went to get laid and I would play poker. Some nights I would of course lose, as you must always sometimes lose at poker, but many nights I won big—or big for then: a month's pay and more in a single night. When my luck had soured I would leave the game for a time and sit and drink Cokes and talk to the whores. Most of them did not know English well but I staggered through with my street Spanish and they talked of families and taking care of children and how to get enough money for the rent and food and sometimes how they had fallen in "love" with young soldiers and gone to live with them in apartments off base as a "regular" for months at a time. They talked of clothes they wanted to buy and clothes they thought were ugly and who was pregnant and who was not and who was pretty and who was not and of birthdays coming and who went crazy at a party and who should not be in the "business" and who would be there forever, or until she was too old, and of houses and weather and families at home in Mexico City or Mazatlán but they never, not once, talked about sex.

It was and is as powerful and as meaningless and of as little true worth as money. It is many things; it is a gift and an expression and (for them) a "business" and a drive and a lust and a way to make babies and ruin kings and queens and it is—according to what I learned talking to the whores—in and of itself completely worthless.

In all the world I have never known people as honest as those prostitutes. Or as compassionate and caring. We became good friends and when I realized how much I hated the army and was thinking of leaving, of running, it was a whore named Maria (as were most of them) who talked me out of it. She sat nude with her large breasts resting on top of a guitar while she sipped Coke and plucked idle chords with her thumb.

"You are up there," she said, meaning from the United States, "and you are smart and sometimes can think. There is everything for you up there if you do not ruin it by breaking the law of the army." So I stayed and while I hated it—and still hate it, the memory of it—I got through it and I would not have without her talking to me, showing me what was me, the silliness of me, and what was reality.

The whores had an understanding of reality that would do all of us good and I was thinking of that in my one-sided conversation with Larry, was thinking I would tell him of it when we stopped for the night when I met the seagull.

CHAPTER EIGHT

THE CANADIAN PRAIRIES south and east of Edmonton are enormous—truly an earthen sea—and staggeringly flat. It's as if a giant ruler scraped the ground for many hundreds of miles up to the gentle rolling mounds of the American prairies.

Distances are always relative. I first crossed the Canadian prairies east to west in 1983 in a 1960 Chevy half-ton pickup pulling a trailer with twenty sled dogs in it, stopping every three hours to let the dogs out to piss and shake down, never getting much over forty miles an hour in the first part of January with temperatures well below zero and wind that worked through every nook and cranny of the truck and found any exposed flesh to freeze. It took years, that trip, or seemed to and if somebody had told me that it would be the *easiest* part of running the Iditarod, I think I would have turned around.

It was, of course, much warmer on the Harley in August, and much faster, if wetter. The rain had followed us and in the immense expanse we could see thunderstorms well ahead of us and sometimes we took back or side roads to miss them, or get on the edge and at least avoid the hail. Hitting hail on a motorcycle doing seventy or eighty miles an hour is something very close to kissing a shotgun.

But it was not on a back road that I met the gull. It might seem strange to meet a seagull anywhere in the center of Canada but I remember that when I was a boy working on the farms in North Dakota, the gulls would follow the tractors when we plowed to eat earthworms from the black dirt as the plow turned them up. Sometimes the gulls would be so thick you could not see six feet back to the plow, and they crapped constantly, covering your clothes and—worse—hitting the red-hot muffler and pipes of the tractor; the wet shit steamed and hissed and the smoke came back into your face. I still cannot see a tractor plowing without smelling the stink of burning gull shit.

The gulls—people on boats call them sky rats—are everywhere they can find food, so I was not surprised to look a mile ahead and see the white bird on the side of the road. It was a four-lane freeway with almost no traffic. The ditches were virtually flat out into the fields, the sky was wide open, if cloudy, and the rain had stopped for the moment.

I checked the back and moved into the left lane and slowed slightly. I'd been doing perhaps eighty and I brought it down to seventy-five or seventy and kept both hands on the bars.

I was now half a mile from the gull. He sat well off to the side of the road pecking at some dead animal. He seemed very settled and besides, he had all of Canada available if he wanted to fly away. There was virtually no other traffic and I checked my mirror. Larry was back there a hundred yards or so. Everything was right.

A quarter mile to the gull.

He still sat on the dead animal. I could see now it was a coyote or dog, from the color of the hair, and the gull was working mightily at pulling something loose.

A hundred yards.

Fifty yards.

When I was twenty yards away the gull suddenly jumped up, flapped wings so big he looked like a white condor and with all of North America to move in he flew directly in front of me. I had one split part of a second to remember that I had seen a man killed by a pheasant coming through a windshield on a car when the gull hit me. Or I hit the gull. Or we hit together. Whatever the exact terminology the effect was the same. Larry said it looked like an instant blizzard. Gull feathers, gull meat, gull shit, and gull guts went everywhere.

He struck just below the headlight and I was doing right at seventy. The blow shook the bike and the carcass—he must had died instantly—bounced around the fork and caught me in the stomach.

I can't imagine what would have happened had he not hit the fork first and given up a large part of the energy of the collision. I would have been swept clean off the bike and most certainly killed, for starters. As it was, it was like getting kicked by a mule. The wind whistled out of my nose and I sucked in air mixed with bits of gull and felt the bike jerk, almost stagger with the blow. I wove across the two lanes before I regained control and brought the Harley over to the shoulder and stopped.

"I hit a gull," I said to Larry as he pulled alongside.

"Are you all right?"

"Yeah." I picked bits of gull out of the engine and front fork, wiped it off my jacket, spit the taste out of my mouth. "The poor bastard jumped right in front of me. He must have wanted to die."

Larry nodded but said nothing and we started back up the road north toward Edmonton. I kept smelling something familiar from the bike, some stink that I couldn't at first place but that triggered an almost palpable feeling of nostalgia in me and I kept remembering things that seemed completely out of place—old bachelor farmers I had known and worked for when I was a boy, chickens, old-fashioned farm meals—and I didn't realize what it was until we stopped for gas and the rich, thick aroma of burning feathers and shit came up from the engine into my face.

It was a smell that went all through my childhood—slaughtering and boiling and plucking chickens on farms—but I thought immediately of Oscar. Oscar was an old—I think he might have been close to eighty-five—bachelor farmer who hired me for part of one summer to help him fence a pasture. The work wasn't hard because Oscar worked slowly and I just had to keep up with him, digging postholes in the rich black ground of Minnesota, and he paid me three dollars a day and room and board but when I came into the kitchen for my first meal I almost gagged.

He had an old wood kitchen stove for cooking and in the summer it made the room almost critically hot. This was well before air-conditioning—hell, Oscar didn't even have electricity—and the heat alone would have nearly dropped me. But the smell that came from the stove was like a wall that hit me at the door, stopped my breath halfway down my throat.

Oscar had been cooking some kind of hash in a large cast-iron pot. (I was to find he cooked once a week and we ate from the pot all week.) He picked the pot up and moved it aside to pull the burner and put more wood in the stove and as my eyes became accustomed to the gloom of the kitchen (I don't believe he had ever washed the windows) I noticed several things.

First, there were chickens, live chickens, all over the place. Eight or ten of them walked around in the kitchen, some sat up on the counters, and others walked in from a second small room. The chickens were not housebroken and there was chicken shit literally everywhere—on the kitchen table, the floors, the counters.

Much of it dried, a lot of it fresh—it was impossible to step on the kitchen floor without hitting it.

Then I saw that the burner on the stove was strangely recessed, a flat disk nearly three inches lower than the rest of the stove top. Since wood cookstoves are flat I thought it a strange design until I found that during the cold winter months as the stove cooled down the chickens would roost on the warm surface to cut the chill of winter nights. They would crap there and over the years the chicken manure built up to a rock-hard surface four inches higher than the steel base. Oscar scraped the burner he used and that kept it lower. The smell was burned and burning chicken shit on the stove top and what makes it astonishing, as I think back on it, is that within a half an hour I was accustomed enough to the stink to sit at the table and eat off a tin plate (he kept them in the cupboard where the chickens couldn't get at them), pushing the birds away while we ate. It is also amazing that while I worked there, I think just over a month, I ate in the kitchen every evening, slept in the small room every night with the sound of the chickens out in the kitchen, and amazingly never had a sick day.

The smell of gull shit on the motor brought Oscar back to me. They say he lived to be ninety-two in that same small shack and in his last year got a bit mean and started to kill and eat the chickens.

We filled the tanks in Edmonton and I noticed that my mileage was much worse than Larry's. I had foolishly installed an after-market carburetor kit in my bike, thinking it would improve my mileage. It did just the opposite. Larry was getting over forty miles a gallon with a stock carburetor and I was barely clearing thirty. Luckily I had a five-gallon tank on mine, while Larry had, I think, a four-gallon tank, so we needed gas at about the same time: every hundred miles, leaving a bit for reserve. I was trusting in faith from what I had heard, that the summer Alaska Highway was not like the winter road. In the winter many of the gas stations close down and there are several places where you need to go well over a hundred miles—at one point nearly two hundred—between fuel stops. We could of course pick up some gas containers and carry extra fuel, and would if we had to, but that was very dangerous—converted the bike into something very like a napalm bomb if you had to lay it over and scraped up a spark—and I hoped we wouldn't have to do it.

I also thought of stopping somewhere and trying to find a mechanic to adjust my carburetor—I didn't have the manual with me and didn't feel confident enough to get in there and start messing around without directions—but I knew no mechanics on the Alaska Highway and here a large jolt of chauvinism stopped me: I wasn't sure I trusted a Canadian mechanic as much as I would an American.

There is, of course, much good and some bad about both countries, and to be sure most of the people I have met in Canada, either there or in Florida (where so many go in the winter that they actually reprint Canadian papers for them there so they don't have to import them from Canada), were charming and gracious and hospitable.

But there have been exceptions and they were particularly difficult when it came to fixing my dog truck, which seemed to break down every fifteen or twenty miles. I was financially torn apart by Canadian mechanics and the work they did was for the large part shoddy and ineffective and I had no desire to turn my Harley over to one of them who might not appreciate the intricacies of motor-road-and-soul.

There is, in America, an almost religious aspect to being a mechanic that does not seem to exist in other countries; a seemingly genetic knowledge of cars, engines, speed, and keeping things running with spit, gum, and a can-do attitude that has permeated and become perhaps the driving force of male American culture. We can, as the man says, Get It Done.

During the Second World War at one point Hitler asked Speer and his other advisers what effect American production would have on airpower if the United States entered the war. At the time Germany was making on the order of two thousand planes a month of all types, some twenty thousand a year, and when Speer told him that America would probably make close to fifty thousand planes a year Hitler thought he was insane. "Nobody could produce at that level..."

In truth at the height of production America was putting out nearly fifty thousand planes a *month*, along with Liberty ships—one every nine days—several thousand tanks, and enough extra to not only feed and take care of themselves but England, France, and Russia as well.

It is still there, this ability, and though I have heard jokes made about greasy-nailed mechanics or dirty farmers in so-called "intellectual" circles, they are usually made by people (or shitheads, according to one trucker I know) who fly in airplanes they cannot build, drive cars they cannot fix, live in houses they cannot construct, and eat food they cannot grow. At some point it becomes very difficult not to think of such people as parasites—fleas, perhaps—who have the gall to live on the very host they ridicule.

So I stayed with my faulty carburetor until Dawson Creek, the official start of the Alaska Highway, where I saw actual gas dripping out of it through the air cleaner and decided I had to try to fix it. I thought it would take hours but there was an adjustment screw that looked promising so I tweaked it and ran the motor a bit and the leak stopped and never came back.

Apparently, I thought at the time, the American mechanical ability was indeed inherited.

CHAPTER NINE

IN TWO RUNNINGS OF THE IDITAROD, in all the hassle of training the dogs, getting them to Alaska, and getting *across* Alaska with them—it is a true nightmare of logistics—what made it all worth the effort (along with finding the love that comes from the dogs) was the country.

When I first crossed the Alaska Range, west of Mount McKinley (or Denali, if you're a politically correct person) I ran with a man named Ted English for a time. Ted had run the race before and with his wife, Lois, was a large help—indeed, I probably could not have done it without their help—and I remember stopping at the top of the range, above timberline at Rainy Pass before starting down, standing with my team amidst the incredible white peaks in a bright midday sun, absolutely stunned by the beauty, and I said to Ted: "My god, look at it. Just *look* at it."

And Ted looked and smiled and made some small comment and went back to work on his dogs as I did but I could not shake it, the beauty. The Navajo have a prayer that says:

> *Above me there is beauty,*
> *Below me there is beauty,*
> *To my left there is beauty,*
> *To my right there is beauty,*
> *To my front there is beauty,*
> *To my rear there is beauty,*
> *There is beauty all around.*

It was that way for me during both Iditarods, for the entire race both times, even in the cut and grind of the storms (it blew so hard at times it would suck your eyelids away from the eyeball and put snow inside), I was steeped in beauty and I thought then, and still think, that everybody should run the Iditarod.

But if you can't—for whatever reason, real or manufactured—there is an easier way. Run the Alaska Highway—preferably on a bike, if not at least in a car or pickup with the GODDAMN WINDOWS OPEN! (More on the reason for this in a bit.)

The same beauty is there on the highway and will be for some time (although the developers and money people are working on ruining it), and whatever you do in your life that you think is important, leave it, borrow or steal the money, and take the trip. Do it now. Stop reading, go out and buy a Harley, and get the hell out before that hot breath you smell on your neck becomes teeth and your life kills you.

If you are lucky the country, or perhaps it should be The Country, will change you, change you for the better, will bring you to what Californians call a "valid reality" and take away the bullshit that seems to be the central core of living a "normal" existence. If you are not lucky the exact same thing will happen; you will no longer be able to stand the humdrum of daily existence and will want more, will want *all* of everything there is to see and hear and have. And maybe that is good luck as well.

After leaving Dawson Creek there is a "tame" stretch for another two hundred or so miles. There are resorts and cabins and motels and tourist traps scattered along the road, and the sides of the highway look manicured and clean with wide shoulders. While the country in the distance—thickly forested with low mountains—is beautiful enough, it still seems somehow controlled.

Then you come down a long, curving hill and cross a bridge over a gorge. This is one of those bridges made of metal with the edges facing up so you can see through if you look straight down, which is very disconcerting on a bike. You seem to be moving over thin air and it's one hell of a long way down. This, coupled with the fact that the little metal ridges grab the tires and make the bike weave back and forth so you are not sure if you are in control, keeps you marvelously alert and wondering if *all* the bridges are like this and just how many more bridges there are before Alaska.

But as you climb away from the bridge in some way everything has changed and you are suddenly on the true Alaska Highway and in The Country and caught up in the beauty. There are of course many beautiful places on the earth and I have been blessed enough to see some of them, more than most. Across Alaska by dog team, sailing on the Pacific, the Sea of Cortés, sailing the fjords of

Alaska; but there is something truly awesome (I hate to use that word because the youth have ruined it but it's so apt) about the northern bush and the way the highway moves through it.

I tend to speed on the Harley, often wrapping it up when the road permits, but the highway is extremely curvy—eighteen hundred miles of very narrow winding mountain roads, often with steep thousand and more foot drops off the side—and so the speed came down. Yet the scenery there perhaps did as much to make me slow, sometimes nearly stop.

What is strange is that I had run the road twice in the winter and somehow missed it all both times. Partly that was the weather—it snowed constantly and we couldn't see more than a hundred yards or so—and partly it was terror. They do not plow the road down to the road surface (either asphalt or gravel, depending on where you are) in the winter but leave an inch or so of packed snow/ice for a surface. Clunking along in an old Chevy pulling a trailer with twenty dogs in it on what amounts to bare ice, making at best fifteen miles an hour with chains grinding away at the rear and meeting semi trucks hauling ass along with their load on narrow blind curves in the middle of a snowstorm with a three-thousand-foot drop and the windows mostly iced over in fifty-below temperatures while remembering that you had long ago lost the right to ask God for help, does not leave much time to look at beautiful scenery. Plus it is dark most of the time in the winter.

It still rained daily. While down in the prairies the rain came in violent thunderstorms that made it nearly impossible to see or keep driving on the Alaska Highway, the rain here came more often in mists or soft showers. We were still always damp and I was developing a really good crop of various fungi, but the gentleness of the rain made the scenery look even more rich, mysterious, and alluring in the thick green laced with mists and low clouds, sometimes below us as we climbed. It seemed as if we were moving through an imaginary world.

The road winds through small and large mountains, many of the peaks snowcapped year-round, and in between because of the elevation of the road, you can see for miles, see until there is nothing to see, see thousands, millions of square miles all as completely wild as it has been for millions of years. The forest has not been logged off (yet) so it is largely virgin growth—perhaps, along with the tropical rain forests (and they are going fast), the last such place on earth. Even the enormous

Siberian forest—it is as large as the entire continental United States—has all been logged off and is on second and in many areas third and even fourth growth.

Here, I thought, staring through my goggles like a boy, here is *old* country. Clean country. God, it was so beautiful that I kept thinking I could just stop, here, and live forever. No, here. Here. Right there by that waterfall. Right here...

And then we hit what would prove to be the worst and most dangerous—potentially lethal—aspect of the whole run.

Motor homes.

CHAPTER
TEN

IN THE WINTER the highway is thick with semi trucks and they drive fast because they must to make money and that creates some risk both to other drivers and to the truckers themselves—I saw several places where they had left the road and gone down thousands of feet, the wrecks left there forever after the bodies have been removed. But the drivers are for the most part professional and know the highway and drive accordingly.

And I'm not going to say that *every* person driving a motor home is a road-ignorant old fart (and I say that *as* an old fart) who couldn't pour piss out of a boot with the instructions written on the heel—a thought that hit me many hundreds of times on the run, along with many less complimentary descriptions.

But most of them on the Alaska Highway seem to fall into that bracket and there are legions of the goddamn things. When the weather comes into summer there must be some genetic code that says everybody with a motor home has to head up the Alaska Highway so they can put one of those stupid bumper stickers (I SURVIVED THE ALASKA HIGHWAY) on their rig. They're like lemmings, except that most of them seem to have less cognitive ability; they are there in their hordes yammering on CB radios, driving—crawling would be a better word—with their windows closed so they cannot see properly, turning into you without looking or signaling, jamming the highway so badly that trucks do not make the run in summer and wait until the weather hardens and the motor homes head for some other place to ruin.

God. I counted forty of them stopped in a row at one point, waiting because the one in front was afraid to go around a curve at more than two or three miles an hour and had backed traffic for over a mile.

Had it been just that they caused delay, it would not have bothered things so much. We were on bikes and could easily scoot around them except on those occasions when luck ran out and there were *two* lines of backed-up vehicles, facing each other, both stopped because of some idiot.

But many of them constituted a danger because of their inability to drive and control their rigs or to pay attention to what they were about. There were many motorcycles on the highway—mostly Honda Gold Wings, some BMWs, and (if I remember correctly) just two other Harleys—and I saw a young man on a BMW starting to pass a motor home when, for absolutely no reason at all, the motor home left its lane, pulled out in front of him, and forced the bike off the road. The motorcycle left the shoulder like a gazelle—the rider somehow holding the front end of the bike up while flipping the bird to the driver of the motor home (who of course did not see it)—to crash twenty feet down in a rocky ditch, bounce twice, and then, spouting dirt and stones, to come roaring up out of the ditch without ever laying the bike down. It was as masterful a bit of driving as I have ever seen, but he was shaken and rightly so. In another two hundred yards there was no ditch but a three- or four-hundred-foot vertical drop and he most certainly would have been killed.

Had the incident been unique, or even infrequent, it would not have been so bad. But it was the rule. We had many close calls and after a time came to view motor homes much as we would stupid cobras—frightening and lethal—and I still can't see one of the damn things without having my nethers pucker up.

There was one advantage to the many traffic jams they caused, however, and that was the fact that when they were all crammed up at a corner waiting for one of them to walk their poodle (is there some code that demands they *all* have poodles?) the rest of the highway is clear. We would—carefully, very carefully—move around them, one at a time, until we passed the one in front and then the highway might be clear for five or six miles, until the next stoppage.

The highway is always under construction or repair. It reminded me of the Golden Gate Bridge in San Francisco; it is said that it is constantly being painted, that as they finish it at one end it's time to start painting the other.

So it is with the highway, especially in Canada—which of course is where the highway mostly runs—and where they are working it is usually dirt. Almost all the highway is asphalted now and much easier to traverse than it must have been when it was all dirt. At all the gas stations and small resorts there are pictures of the making of the highway, which was started in 1942, and the terrain must have been incredibly daunting to the men who worked the road then. Equipment was limited, the weather was often appalling, and simply the concept—making a highway across nearly two thousand miles of raw, mountainous wilderness—was beyond comprehension for many of the workers. It's one thing to take a trail on foot or by dog team as was often the case in that country, but to make a usable year-round road through some of the mountains, swamps, and bogs that they had to work through borders on the impossible. That they did it is certainly a testimony to working men; surely it classes among the wonders of the world.

It is now almost completely domesticated (clearly so or the hordes of motor homes couldn't make the trip), but when we made the run, there were probably seventy miles of unimproved or dirt roads. Had they all been in one place it would have been simpler, but they came a mile here, two miles there, six miles somewhere else. There were warning signs for these short stretches, but it was raining almost constantly, which obscured vision through my goggles, and while there were warnings there was usually just one sign.

The upshot was that on several occasions, I would come rumbling around a corner at fifty or so, my goggles hazy with water, and miss the sign completely and suddenly find myself in three inches of mud, on a bike leaning into a curve with a total weight of something near seven hundred pounds.

The effects were predictable, immediate, and very dramatic. A street Harley is a marvelous instrument on a surfaced highway; comfortable, powerful, well balanced, and easy to ride. On a slick mud road, leaned over for a turn, the same bike turns into a monster that completely defies control of any kind and is seemingly devoted to one thing and one thing only—to get over on its side and stick your ass and face into the mud as fast as it can and as hard as it can.

The first time I made a surprise dump on the Alaska Highway I had mud in my ears, in my eyes, jammed up into my pant leg, packed into my mouth, squeezed *inside* my gloves and covering my whole body and all the bike as well. I couldn't see and was just clawing the muck out of my eyes when Larry came running up, his face full of concern.

"Are you all right?"

I said something pithy and descriptive, then added, "Would you help me lift the bike off my leg please?"

Larry did and I cleaned mud for half an hour or so, checked to see that nothing was broken—on me or the bike—started the engine again (it had stopped when I hit the kill switch on the handgrip as I went over), straddled the bike, put it in gear, then I *eased* the clutch out until the power started to turn the back wheel.

And I promptly went over again, this time in the other direction.

I once ran a dog team across a lake and in the middle hit bare new ice, about as slick as glass with oil on it, and watched the dogs scrabble and claw and slip and fall until they had worked the sled back to the snowpack.

It was the same for me now. Having been down once, then again, it seemed like the Harley *wanted* to be on its side. I could *not* get the damn thing to stay up. Larry helped me get the bike upright again, I would go down again, then up and down, and while Larry was very kind and patient, I know he must have been thinking that a set of training wheels wouldn't be out of line, or that it was going to take us a hell of a long time to get to Alaska going six feet at a time.

Finally I evolved a system that seemed to work. I would get the bike ready, put it in gear, ease the clutch out, and then not try to correct but go where the bike wanted to take me. It was in correcting that I caused it to fall; throwing my weight from side to side or turning the front wheel rapidly were sure ways to bite—and I do mean *bite*—the dirt.

Of course this made for some interesting side trips, weaving back and forth, letting the bike decide where to go, but I found that if I merely *thought* about the correction and didn't allow myself to do it, the bike would respond. (I know how that sounds—that I was probably a candidate for some form of therapy—but it worked.) Larry never fell. Not once. While I was down so often you could have used me for a plow and while he would explain how he stayed upright, I couldn't get it to work very well and finally wrote it off to the fact that we probably had different centers of gravity, or that my mud karma was cosmically doomed.

I was, however, not alone. At one section of road, during a particularly heavy downpour we came upon an old man—we found later he was close to eighty—with a Honda Gold Wing lying over on its side in the mud. Gold Wings are a good bike—not a Harley, but a good bike—with amenities (adjustable shock absorbers, cruise control, front- and backseat stereo speakers, a ventilation system to blow hot air on your cold legs) but they have a relatively high center of gravity (as does the BMW and most other bikes) and are a large, heavy six-cylinder motorcycle. The upshot of all this is that they tend to want to stay down when they get down and they are brutes to get back on their feet.

In this case the problem was compounded by the fact that the bike had tipped on the shoulder when the kickstand had sunk in the mud and dropped not just over but over and down the ditch bank slightly so it was below center.

We stopped to help and two other men were there, plus the driver, and it was all we could do to get the bike back on its wheels.

"I always took a Harley," the old man said. "I do this every year and I always took a Harley but this year I decided to go with a Gold Wing because the Harley took too much work and maintenance. Shit . . ."

This was a particularly bad stretch of road construction—actually the worst we were to encounter— with earthmovers and other heavy equipment roaring past, throwing gouts of mud in the air, and rain pouring down in a steady stream. I, of course, had fallen and would nearly fall several more times, when I hit six-inch-deep ruts in the mud, and I expended most of the cursing

I was allowed in my life over the next seven miles of muck. I noticed as we progressed that there were several places where single-wheel tracks went off to the side of the shoulder and there would be sitzmarks in the mud where a bike was laid over and I thought with true pity that here was a man who dropped his bike more than even I did.

Later that day we stopped at a gas station next to a small cafe. The road was back to a good surface and had been that way for forty or fifty miles, so the taste of mud was nearly out of my mouth and mind. As we pulled into the station I saw a Harley Dresser off to the side. It was virtually slathered with mud and sitting on the back, in the comfortable seat with the little armrests, was a young woman equally mud-covered, wearing a helmet with a Plexiglas bubble that was mud-encrusted except for a semi-opaque smear where her eyes were.

Usually people are more than ready to get off their bikes when they get to a station, especially in rain, and after being laid over a few times in mud—as this Dresser had obviously been—and *more* especially if there is a cafe where hot food and coffee are available.

But she sat there stiff-backed and rigid, staring straight ahead, and did not answer me when I said hello.

I felt that I should stop and talk to her, help her in some way, but she seemed to want to be by herself and when she looked away I saw in the side of the bubble and could tell she was absolutely furious, purple with rage.

I left her and we went inside to have some coffee and a bite and to get out of the cold (it felt on the edge of snowing) and I was surprised to see a young man sitting at the counter in mud-spattered rain gear, his helmet on the stool next to him, eating a full-size meal (most of the cafes served wonderful home-cooked food in enormous quantities).

Clearly he was with the young woman—there was only the one motorcycle other than ours outside—and he nodded and smiled when we sat down. "Going up or down?" he asked—it was the most-asked question we heard on the run.

"Up," I said, "then down."

"We're going up," he said, taking a mouthful of food. "If she's still on the bike. Is she still out there?"

I nodded. "The woman on the bike? Yes, she's still there. Sitting there."

"It's our honeymoon," he said. "We're from Boston."

"She seems . . . upset."

He nodded. "She got a little scared the third time we went down. Back in the mud. She says she's not getting off the bike until we get to an airport, then she's flying back. It's not quite what she expected."

It never is, I thought. They say no marriage survives three Iditarods and that La Paz, Mexico, is the divorce capital for sailors who take their wives down Baja and around Cabo San Lucas and hit the northwesterlies coming out of the Sea of Cortés for the first time. Perhaps running a bike up the Alaska Highway when it is raining (and when is it not?) should be in the same league.

It is never quite what they expect and when it goes sour—and many of the rough things to do seem to go sour easily—the effect is somehow worse on the women. It is of course the man's fault for not telling the truth, the whole truth, and nothing but the truth about the possible difficulties involved.

"I went down a few times," I said. "It must be hard riding a bike through that mud carrying double." Damn near impossible, I thought.

"Yeah, I guess I should have told her it would be a little rough," he said, smiling around a forkful of mashed potatoes. "But then hell, she wouldn't have come at all. She'll get over it."

No, I thought. She won't. They say they will and they might mean it when they say it but they don't get over it, not ever. They save it for later when you aren't ready for it. Maybe years. Then they drop it on you like a bomb. At least that had been my experience. But then I thought how negative that was, the thinking, and that probably after a time she would lose the bitterness of this and forget that it happened on her honeymoon and that he had lied to her, Lied to Her on Her Honeymoon.

But we were there a good half hour, and I watched the young man finish his lunch—he didn't seem to hurry—and when we went out and gassed our bikes and left, she was still sitting on the bike, stiff, waiting for him to come out and get her to an airport. Considering that the next true airport wasn't until White Horse, up in the Yukon, she had a good long ride to go on the back of that Harley and there were to be many more patches of mud.

CHAPTER ELEVEN

THE COUNTRY GREW, if anything, wilder. We came to
the gas station that marked the highest pass on the Alaska
Highway and I remember thinking when I made the run
in the winter hauling dogs that surely this must be the
hardest part and that it was mostly over now. It wasn't.
With the old truck we had four more days of driving through snowstorms and fifty- to sixty-below-zero
weather just to reach Alaska, not to mention getting to
Anchorage or starting the race or running the dogs to
Nome or flying them back to Anchorage from Nome or
returning with them to Minnesota. I still have nightmares

about the logistics of running dogs; horror dreams of endless paperwork and hassling with airlines and car rental people and rude customs officials at border crossings, terrible dreams where the work is endless and never accomplishes anything. They are often accompanied by the dream that I have become drunk and reenlisted in the army (the army was not my favorite place) and do not realize it until I get off the troop train and a sergeant with a body like Hercules and a head the size of an orange is calling me a fucking maggot and telling me to give him two thousand push-ups.

It was so much more...peaceful...on the bike with just the roar of the wind and the solid thunk of the engine beneath me.

The more you are outside the more difficult it becomes to be inside. Of course the reverse is true as well but once you have made the jump from inside all the time to living—not just going for a walk but actually living—outside a building it is nearly impossible to be an inside person again. In hotels in New York City on business trips, I still sleep with the window wide open—in the winter as well as summer—and if I can't see the sun or the sky I feel lost, emotionally, psychologically, and physically lost. I felt it strongly now on the ride, the need to be outside and never be inside again—never—to always have this wind and this rain, and I thought again of telling Larry about it but the day passed and other things happened and it slipped away.

We came on an accident. In the literal middle of a literal nowhere in the Yukon, we came around a corner and there was a Toyota van off to the side of the road, burned to the ground. Had I not seen it I don't think I would have believed it. Everything on that van that was possible to burn had gone so that all that was left was the metal shell which was sitting on the steel rims—even the tires burned off—and I thought that whoever had been in the still-smoldering wreck was surely dead.

But as we came a little closer I saw a family standing off to the side—a man, woman, and child—with the bewildered look that comes on people after an accident. We stopped of course but there was little we could do except commiserate. "I was just driving down the road and she started to smoke," the man said. "I pulled over and there were some flames and we got out and that was it—the whole thing went up."

The highway was well traveled—constantly traveled, to be more accurate—and other people with vehicles were showing up as we stood there and (unlike some highways down in the States) almost everybody stopped to help so we moved on but I couldn't get the look on their faces out of my mind.

I had worked on a volunteer ambulance for a time in eastern Colorado. We got called for car wrecks and farm accidents, and it was often grisly work. Modern cars are not made very strongly and move at very high speeds, and people are evidently becoming less and less adept at driving. The upshot is that accidents seem to be more violent and do more damage all the time—especially if people do not use seat belts, which was most often the case. When I rode the ambulance there were many nights I could not sleep and some accidents that are still difficult to think about, especially those involving children. I saw highway patrol officers crying openly at some wrecks and always, always there was that same bewildered look on the people who survived as on the people in the burned van.

The refugee look, I heard it called. Once they had had something, now they had nothing. I had seen that look many times on many faces, but the one that stopped me, made me quit answering the siren, was a young man named Mike Vaughn who worked on a ranch. Mike picked up a long piece of aluminum irrigation pipe to swing it over, pulled it too high, and hit an electrical high line with several thousand volts passing overhead. It killed him instantly and we arrived with the ambulance perhaps fifteen minutes later, too late to do anything. But his wife and two children were there and they stood and watched us and we could not stop working on him though we knew he was gone, could not stop until over an hour had passed and the helicopter from Denver finally arrived, could not stop doing CPR because every time we looked up there were the kids, standing there, looking down at their father and the wife, standing there.

Later she sent me a small card, a sweet card thanking me for our effort, and I sat looking at the note thinking how utterly, miserably unfair all of life really is and had the anger that came when I first saw him dead there on the ground, anger at nobody, at everybody, anger at waste, anger at God.

That night we pulled over at one of the dozens of small highway wide-stops that lie along the highway. They all look the same. A log building with a cafe, some other newer buildings made of plywood and paint in a kind of 1950s effort to get something up, quick, and start getting money from the people who come through. There seemed to be little thought spent on architectural beauty and much thought on function. A roof, walls, a window or two, and some oddly colored paint—the kind of color that comes from having paint left over from other jobs.

There was a woman working there. I do not remember her name, or even if she gave it, but she was the type of woman who works in cafes waiting tables and cooking—they all seemed to be named Madge, or Carla—that makes you think of how wonderful women can really be. Resourceful, with humor in her eyes and a hard little edge so you knew she wouldn't take any bullshit from anybody she didn't like, but feminine. Forty, perhaps, single, and still pretty in a burnished kind of way, and she traded banter with Larry and then with me—though she liked Larry more—and asked about our "scooters."

She said that she had once ridden but then her old man moved on and she had to raise the kids and wound up on the highway. But she missed the ride, she said, and she was telling the truth because her eyes misted a bit and she looked out the window at the rain with a genuine longing in her eyes; of course that could have been just wanting to get out of the bush and off the highway. We met many like that—there to get some money and get the hell out.

Larry joked about taking her with us and she studied him for a moment, thinking seriously, and I thought, she's going to do it, she's going to come and I was sure Larry would have put her on the back. Then the look was gone and she shook her head and went back to work and we finished eating and went to our plywood cubicle (motel room) to clean the bikes and get ready for the next day. As I dozed off I realized that talking with her had taken the scenes of accidents out of my mind, which brought them back, and the room felt close, after the wind of the day, and I couldn't sleep.

I listened to Larry breathing for a time, then went outside and watched the pale-lighted night sky until something on the order of four million mosquitoes found me and drove me back inside to sleep. It is one thing to say you are going to live outside all the time. It is something else to do it. Especially when there are creatures that want to drink your blood.

There were many women working on the highway on the Canadian portion and it was strange to see them. In the States, women work on the highway but they are usually flag persons. In Canada they were running the machinery, using shovels, driving gravel trucks, spitting, farting, and scratching just like the men. I did not see any controversy up there about it—there was much more about what Americans should or should not do in Canada than there was about hiring women to do what was formerly considered men's work—and it was refreshing to see them busting their asses on shovels and scrapers.

The controversy is of course silly. There should be an Equal Rights Amendment to the Constitution. If somebody can do a job, they should do it, regardless of sex, and for equal pay—even the jobs they don't want to do. For instance, all healthy men in the United States have a hidden eight-year military obligation. It used to be two years of active service and six in training reserves in case we needed to be called up in a hurry. We did not have a choice. We were not asked if we wanted to do it or not and we were not given a choice as to what we would do in the military. They gave us a rifle and taught us to kill other men whether we wanted to do it or not and that was it. We simply had to. It was the law. If you chose not to do it you went to prison for two to ten years and many of the men who did it against their will, fulfilled their obligation, were then taken to strange places and hundreds of thousands of them were slaughtered in ways that are unspeakable. (Modern weapons—from the Civil War on and especially from the Second World War to the present—are staggering in their destructive ability. We now have antipersonnel weapons that can vaporize a human.) This system can be reenergized in moments, the draft reinstated, and of course it should apply to all citizens. I was paid seventy-eight dollars a month for three years, eight months, twenty-one days, and nine hours (I was extended eight months by JFK to fight in Cuba if necessary) and would gladly have given my job to somebody else.

I watched a young woman raking gravel by hand into a pothole while a man leaned on a shovel watching her and another man—honest to god—waved a flag at me to slow down. I thought of a friend who had fought in Vietnam in the marines. Old now—we're all old now and as misunderstood as dinosaurs—he shook his head and sighed about the effort to pass the ERA and said, "I don't care, I just don't think I could order a woman to take the point, and if she can't take point it's just not equal." Point, for those who are not acquainted with infantry tactics, is the person in an infantry squad who walks in the foremost position; it is this person who is first hit if the enemy is contacted and the person who walks point is rotated because it is so dangerous in action. I talked to many men who—though dubious about it— thought women should be given the chance the fight in combat if they could hack it, but they all, almost to a man, said they didn't think they could order a woman to walk point. It seemed almost genetic, like they could not personally order a woman to die. Women of course have fought in wars; in the Soviet Union they fought in the infantry and as fighter pilots, and did well. One woman sniper killed over a hundred Germans during the siege of Stalingrad.

But the feeling is still there, I think, that it would be difficult to tell a woman she had to die so that the men could live, which is really what point is all about. Another thing to ask Larry, I thought, accelerating away from the potholes, but about then we hit the worst part of the highway and I damn near died without thinking or believing that it was happening.

CHAPTER TWELVE

THE PHYSICS OF RIDING A HARLEY are at the same time very straightforward and extremely complex and vary with speed, weather, wind, road surface, and other drivers.

At a slow speed, for instance, just after accelerating from a stop, to turn the bike left you pull the left handlebar and the bike follows the wheel. At a certain point in acceleration, however, it flops and to turn the bike left you put pulling pressure on the *right* handlebar. This point varies with bikes and is easily and quickly learned but it is just one thing.

Another point to consider is that when the bike is at highway speed it tends to be very stable. The spinning wheels become a form of gyroscope and "lock" the bike into position so that it tends to stay upright and will handle even a mild collision—hitting a small animal or object—without going down. (Although I know a man who hit a cow broadside at night, and he did not stay upright. Neither, he said, did the cow.)

Then too there is the fact that in a tight turn the bike is leaned well over and the wheels lose traction and if you accelerate out of the turn you lose more traction still and if there is dust or dirt or loose gravel or moisture or oil in the turn still more traction is lost and if a gust of wind hits you right then when the traction is low and you have slowed and lost the gyro action and God is not on your side and you look up to see a motor home coming at you...

Well, you get the picture. Everything that once was simple becomes very complicated very fast and that is essentially what happened to me.

There was a long straightaway and the rain had let up a bit. In front of me a couple of hundred yards there was—of course—a motor home. I checked my mirror and saw Larry back there, no other traffic coming, so I cracked the handgrip and took her up to seventy-five to whip around the motor home and back in. A straight pass, clean, no traffic.

Sometime during the winter when they were plowing the road the grader had left the corner of the blade down too much and gouged the road surface in a two-inch-deep groove that started at the center line and moved out to the shoulder on the left side of the road (as I faced it), which was made up of soft wet dirt and thick mud.

I hit this groove just as I caught seventy-five and started around the motor home and the wheels dropped into it like they had found a home. I decelerated instantly but the groove took me away from the highway and toward the muddy shoulder and a twenty-foot drop so fast, so completely instantly that I didn't even have time for fear. One part of a second I was there, the next I had no control of the bike and was heading off to the side at over seventy miles an hour.

The groove paid out about one inch—no more than that—from the edge of the asphalt and the bike ran there, hung there, teetered there, while I looked down in growing horror for what seemed like miles. I was caught in one of those off-balance things where you can't move the way you need to move because it will make the bike turn the wrong way and I could do nothing but stare down at the front wheel, still spinning at seventy a bare inch from the mud and then it moved, just a hair closer and I shifted my weight and tipped it away and it came out and I passed the motor home and could not stop shaking, thinking of it, for miles; could see nothing but the mud and my tire. It is in this way that people die, I thought. They are perfectly sober and there is good visibility and the road is dry and the bike is in good shape and nothing can go wrong and they splatter themselves all over the landscape.

"I thought you were going to die." Larry had seen the whole thing and shook his head when we stopped for gas. "You just headed for the ditch. I thought you'd had a heart attack or something."

"There was a groove," I said. "My wheel got caught in the groove." As if, I thought, it made any difference in the whole world. One minute you're there, the next you're gone. The groove didn't matter, the road didn't matter. If I'd passed an instant later or sooner the groove wouldn't have been there to catch me; if the bike had gone another inch to the left it would have hit the ditch and plowed me in at seventy. "It doesn't matter."

Larry nodded and we rode again and entered the last two hundred miles before the Alaska state line where we found out about the wonderful world of frost heaves.

There is a long, relatively flat run there where the highway runs through muskeg and spruce swamps. It is straight and low, with little or no mountain driving, and as I came off a ridge I looked out and could see the road stretching away flat for miles. It was the first time in over a thousand miles of winding turns that the road lined out and as I came into the flats I locked the throttle down at about eighty, leaned back against the sleeping bag and prepared to relax and stretch my legs on the outside pegs.

The world suddenly went mad.

The bike simply dropped out from beneath me. One instant I was sitting back and down in the seat, leaning against the bag, and the next the bike was below me—my ass literally in midair—and just as gravity kicked in and I started down like a rock the bike came back up and slapped my hind end so hard it knocked the air out of me. Simultaneously the front shocks bottomed with a tooth-jarring jolt and the bike, the whole bike with me on it, left the ground and flew through the air at eighty miles an hour. I had just time to wonder what in hell was happening when I crashed back down to the highway, wobbled a bit and regained balance, hands still on the grips.

I had honest to god not seen it coming, had no idea, and I looked in the mirror just in time to see Larry hit the hole and get airborne. It was a massive dip, at least four feet deep and of very short duration, and with the light as it was, there had been no indication, no warning, nothing to see but flat highway out ahead.

In that swamp country the ground froze solid each winter, then thawed in the spring and summer and re-froze and thawed—for fifty-plus years—expanding as it froze, contracting as it thawed, pushing the road up and down each time. The problem is that it isn't an even process and the land is very flexible, pushes up here, sinks there, and the highway follows it.

It was a nightmare. I just couldn't see them and there were dozens, hundreds of sudden dips. The only solution was to drive slowly and just sink with them when they came. I suddenly noted ahead of me a shower of sparks when a motor home caught one with the front bumper—the edges were gouged where the motor homes dug in—and then I hit one I hadn't seen because I was watching the motor home.

You couldn't take your eyes off the road, not for an instant. Sometimes they were close, sometimes farther apart, but never predictable and if you relaxed you were certain to get nailed.

CHAPTER THIRTEEN

WE HAD GONE PERHAPS FIFTY MILES in the frost heaves when we came on a small gas station and stopped for gas. We cut our engines, filled the tanks, had a Coke and a piss, and were ready to go.

Larry's bike wouldn't start. It was just flat dead. The ignition turned on, the lights came on, but nothing got to the engine and the starter wouldn't turn over.

We looked everywhere for a loose wire and couldn't find anything and finally he shrugged. "I'll start it on the hill and if it runs keep it going until we stop for the night. It's probably something simple."

The station was on a slight hill and he got the bike rolling, popped it in gear and it fired right off and ran fine for another hundred miles when we stopped for the night at a plywood motel. Light was not a problem—there were only about two hours of dark in the day—so we ate first and then looked at the bike.

After he took the seat off and we pulled and pushed he found a wrapped tube harness of four or five wires that looked as if it had been torn in half and then somehow been rubbing against the tire. At first we could not find where the wires were to go but then found a female plug on the engine casing that had a similar wire coming from it, also torn in half and also looking as if it had been rubbing against the tire.

Since the wires were too short by six or seven inches to reach the tire it didn't make any sense. I had a roll of tape and we had tools and Larry spliced the wires and the next morning the bike started straight off and we went back to the highway.

We stopped for gas two hours along the way and it was the same thing. The bike wouldn't start and when Larry pulled the seat the wires were parted at the splice and frayed on the ends. He fixed it again and when we stopped that evening it was the same once more. It was ridiculous, impossible.

"A gremlin," he said. "Some little monster that gets in there..."

"We'll get to Fairbanks day after tomorrow," I said. "There's a Harley dealer there. Maybe they'll know what to do."

"I don't know how they can see more than us. The wire is getting worn through but it can't be reaching anywhere that would wear on it."

"And it just started happening."

He nodded. "There was no trouble at all until we hit this last stretch of road."

"The frost heaves."

But they weren't doing anything that wasn't happening before, and the heaves couldn't make the wire longer. It just didn't make sense.

Fairbanks happened on us gradually. We came upon cabins and homes miles before the town, found a motel more or less in the middle of town—a lot of logs and varnished poles for staircases, a tiny basement room where we had to duct-tape the window shades because it was still so light late at night that we couldn't sleep.

The next morning we were having coffee and Larry looked at me and said, "Now what?"

"What do you mean?"

"Well, we made Alaska. Now what?"

I thought for a minute, then shrugged. "What the hell, let's go home."

He smiled and nodded and that was it. We finished breakfast—we'd been in Fairbanks for less than ten hours—and went out to our bikes. Larry had rewired his the night before when the problem recurred and when they started we quickly found the Harley dealer and they were most friendly. Larry bought a Harley tee shirt there—he wanted a Harley tee shirt from every Harley dealer we stopped at for a collection—but as Larry had predicted they couldn't help with the problem any more than we could. In fact Larry figured it out on the way back, when it happened again and the ensuing short caused his starter to engage at seventy miles an hour. I heard the noise a hundred feet in front of him, over the sound of my own motor, a horrible grinding that made my teeth loose.

While in the States he had taken his bike in for a recall on a solenoid and when they rewired the bike they'd run the wire harness over a metal brace under the seat. Normally it was all right but when he hit a particularly deep frost heave his weight slammed down on the seat, which slammed down on the wire harness, cutting all the wires, and they dropped down and caught mud and looked as if they had frayed on the tire. It was a simple matter of rerouting the wire harness under the tube instead of over it—but the last mess ruined his starter, though it lasted until we got home.

Larry needed to get his bike serviced in Fairbanks, which was going to take several hours (they had some work to do before they could get to his), and I started to wait with him.

But there was a problem with motels. There were very few of them and if you didn't get to them early in the day—before two or three in the afternoon—they were likely to be filled. We were getting a late start and if I waited for Larry we might not get a room down toward Haines Junction so I decided to go on ahead and he could catch up as soon as they finished with his bike. That way I could get a room and be waiting when he came.

There was another reason that I wanted to get going. I had become uncomfortable in Fairbanks. It was not the town, nor the people. Everybody was wonderfully courteous and friendly and as I had learned before when I came up to run the Iditarod, there is nothing on the planet to match Alaskan hospitality.

There was some other reason that I couldn't at first

pin down. A kind of unsettledness had come over me, an uneasiness with stopping, with not running; I felt caged, held, confined to some restriction I didn't at first understand, and only felt at ease when I was moving, rolling, riding.

I left Fairbanks alone, heading back down the highway. For a change—and only for that afternoon—the sun came out and it was a glorious day, the leaves on the birch trees shading the road in dappled green, like riding through an impressionist painting, and I must have gone seventy or eighty miles before it came to me; what was bothering me.

I was coursing.

God knows I had seen it often enough. I'd watched wolves do it when they hunted and dogs when they ran and men and some women do it with their eyes when they die and I should have known what it was when I did it.

To seek. Not to find, not to end but to always seek a beginning. That was what the trip had become for me—as the Iditarods had been, and all of my life had been, though I had not seen it, not understood it—a pilgrimage only to seek. And Fairbanks had in some way come to mean an end to me, of me. We had wanted to run the Alaska Highway with Harleys. We had done it and now it was over, at least one way, and I could not abide the ending, could not stand to be done.

I could not stop it, could never stop it and I knew it then, knew I had to leave, to get moving again, to seek, to continue the run for the rest of my life and that if I stopped, even for a moment, "it" would catch up with me—whatever "it" was—and I would stop. Stop forever.

And so the roll back down the highway came, and bad curves with mud and more motor homes filled with red-faced men and women bitching about the cost of gas but not seeing the country; and a herd of mountain goats we had to thread our way through, so tame we had to push them out of the way with our feet as we moved the bikes ahead; and a Mountie who gave us a ticket for speeding and passing motor homes illegally; and country so beautiful it was hard to look at and more rain, god for the rain and finally, after crossing back into the States and Montana and Wyoming, finally one perfect Harley day.

We slept in Cheyenne, Wyoming, a full eight hundred miles from home, and left at four in the morning to make the run in one more day in rain on the edge of snow which followed us across Colorado, wet and cold, until

Raton Pass in northern New Mexico. There, about one in the afternoon the sun came out, brilliant and hot as only a desert sun in August could be, came out like an old friend and we stripped down to tee shirts and jeans and I leaned back and wrapped the throttle all the way out, put my boots on the outside pegs and let the hot air blow up my pant legs and dry my body and warm my bones and crossed four hundred miles of New Mexico that way, leaning back against the sleeping bag with a ninety-mile-an-hour hot wind on my face knowing that no matter what came it would not end.

The run would never end.

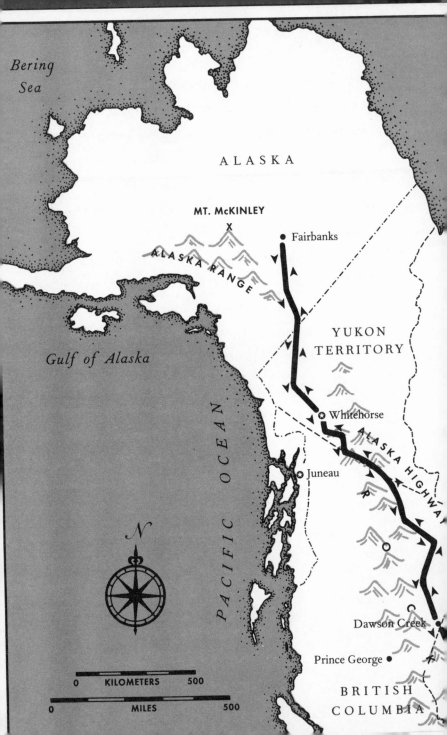

STORAGE